LOSER TAKES ALL

Bud Adams,
Bad Football,
& Big Business

ED FOWLER

LONGSTREET PRESS
Atlanta, Georgia

Published by
LONGSTREET PRESS, INC.
A subsidiary of Cox Newspapers
A subsidiary of Cox Enterprises, Inc.
2140 Newmarket Parkway
Suite 122
Marietta, GA 30067

Printed in the United States of America

1st printing 1997

Library of Congress Catalog Card Number: 97-71937

ISBN: 1-56352-432-5

Jacket design by Burtch Bennett Hunter
Electronic film prep by OGI, Forest Park, GA
Book design by Graham & Company Graphics, Inc.

FOR MARJORIE

ACKNOWLEDGMENTS

With thanks to John McClain and John Williams of the *Houston Chronicle* for their reporting of the Oilers and the move to Tennessee, to Margaret Jamison of the *Chronicle* library for her research assistance on this project, and to Bud Adams, Ladd Herzeg, and Jerry Glanville for all the laughs.

CONTENTS

LOSER
TAKES
ALL

FOREWORD

Houston can be an ornery town. It's a strange thing, but even though just about everybody comes from someplace else, it's a town with a mind of its own. During the oil boom of the 1970s, settlers in the energy capital had a message for countrymen on the East and West Coasts who didn't want their pretty, white beaches menaced by oil spills. They put it on a bumper sticker: "Let the bastards freeze in the dark."

Little wonder. The people who shaped the place never shied from a fight. Some of them cracked a longneck over a bedpost at sunrise and went looking for one. For skin, they wore rawhide, baked to the murky brown of Mexican butter. They went searching for "dead dinosaurs," as they liked to call oil, and were ready to take on a live one if it got in their way. Men died poking holes in the ground, sometimes of most unnatural causes. Men became rich, and broke on their butts, and rich again.

Wildcatters followed cowboys over the horizon as conglomerates leased up every square inch of dirt that might cover a dropper's worth of Vaseline. Houston changed, and it didn't. The skyline evolved into a swoop of gleaming zigs and zags hailed by critics of architecture as an art form. The arts blossomed, in some cases to a world-class level. The Medical Center lured esteemed surgeons and researchers. Houston found a veneer. The wildcatters went in for manicures.

They didn't scour the earth for oil any longer. Engineers and bureaucrats with MBAs stacked on top of one another in office towers assumed that role, but the spirit survived. Up Interstate 45 just 240 miles, Texas' second city, Dallas, became known for banking and fashion and a silly soap opera. Houston didn't care, or didn't want the cosmopolitan gloss badly enough to surrender its feisty nature. Fighters continued to define the city, lawyers such as Percy Foreman, Leon Jaworski, Richard "Racehorse" Haynes, and Joe Jamail who would wade into an unwinnable murder case or a corporate giant and emerge with bloody knuckles raised to the sky. John Connally stepped out of their ranks and into politics, and he could squint into the sun with the best of 'em.

Then came the astronauts, those space cowboys who refused to let gravity pin them down. If not for their degrees and their ranks, they would have been stock-car drivers hauling screaming moonshine on the back roads around Talladega or Darlington. Tom Wolfe told their tale of "drivin' and drinkin', drinkin' and drivin'," and we learned that some of them liked honey with their whiskey, and that the devout John Glenn might have been their mascot but was never their captain.

Gifted surgeons kept their gloves on, but men such as Denton Cooley and Michael De Bakey pushed the envelope in their own way.

Muhammad Ali lived in Houston when he was duking it out with Selective Service. Howard Hughes had a presence. Still does, of sorts, in a cemetery. Municipal zoning still does not. Into this vibrant and untamed land stumbled Bud.

LOVE AND MONEY

Kenneth Stanley Adams, Jr., son of Boots, arrived quite by accident as a young man with big dreams and a charter membership in the Lucky Sperm Club. Daddy, the chairman of Phillips 66, gave him a stake Bud has described as modest. If that's the case, modesty becomes him. Over five decades, he has left his footprints in gasoline distribution, oil production, ranching, banking, real estate, automobile sales, pig farming, and other enterprises, often with marked success.

But not always. With Lamar Hunt, Adams founded the American Football League. By himself, he started the Houston Oilers. Also single-handedly, he operated for 37 years a franchise with a franchise on turmoil, intrigue, back-stabbing, and buffoonery that might have been loved by Houston if not for the last. Bud spent so much time clowning around he forgot to win. Not once has anyone associated with his team attended a Super Bowl without a ticket.

As civic embarrassments go, it would be unfair to say the rotund little man with the flinty eyes and slicked-down strings of hair has waddled into a class all his own. For years, he has shared a table at National Football League owners meetings with the likes of Al Davis, Robert Irsay, and Bill Bidwill. None of them, however, operated in one city for nearly so long without finding the route to the Super Bowl. Likewise, those in Houston who grouse that "Bottom-Line Bud," as he was christened years ago, never wanted to win take a far too charitable view. It's more likely he has never figured out how.

Over the years, in fact, the Oilers' player payroll has ranked often among the top ten in the league. It was seldom the cash that was lacking, only the know-how. Fans clung desperately to the rationale that Bud was a miser, perhaps because it was easier to believe he would one day reinvent himself as a big spender than as a shrewd manager.

But the fans have had to let go — of their hopes and of their team. Bud has left and has taken his Oilers with him

If smugness is one of the NFL's dominant characteristics, astute observers shouldn't allow it to crowd cynicism out of their picture of the No Fun League. One of the owners' criteria for allowing a franchise to relocate is a lack of local support, that quaint notion peculiar to sports. When a businessman such as Adams foists off on the public an inferior product for almost four decades and the public fails to respond, fans are tried and convicted of an incapacity to love. They are found to be morally bankrupt and unworthy of the sculptured young competitors who strive mightily to do them proud, at least until they're eligible for free agency. The NFL judged Houston on the support standard and, naturally, found the city wanting when a just verdict would have been quite different, to wit:

Suckers!

Before Adams began his courtship with Nashville, he mounted a campaign for a new stadium in Houston. The genesis of his wish for a fancier castle grew out of a changing of the guard. Adams long has kept a Rasputin at his elbow, declaring as far back as the 1960s that he was bowing out of the operation of the football team and turning it over to general manager Don Klosterman. In short order, he canned Klosterman for spending too freely, but by the late 1970s Adams had fingered a fellow ideally suited to his purposes, one with no principles whatsoever. His name was Ladd Herzeg, whose character was vividly illustrated when he dropped his pants and mooned a wedding reception at the team hotel the night before a game with Buffalo.

The new Rasputin had been anointed, and he was about to block out the sun in Bud's realm. Like his employer, Herzeg was a man of impressive girth. Unlike Adams, he joked about his belly. "My friends ask me why I stay married," he quipped. "I tell them without my wife around I'd never get my shoes tied." This romantic fool soon was installed as second-in-command in each of Adams's companies. Throughout the 1980s, the owner even stayed home when his fellow moguls held league meetings, sending his deputy in his stead. In Houston, Adams virtually vanished from public view, rarely so much as making a post-game appearance in the locker room. For a time, his reticence seemed a relief. Then Houston got to know Ladd Herzeg.

Top to bottom, the general manager engineered the Great Jacksonville Scam of ten years ago, a sort of prefiguration of the move to Nashville. Working the Jacksonville deal, he occasionally even hustled his newly agoraphobic boss out of his mansion in River Oaks — the Bel Air of Houston — for a quick hop to Florida on his private jet. In Jacksonville, Adams beamed into every camera and pressed the flesh of every politician, inspected the Gator Bowl, and listened intently to the city's grand plans for pro football. Houston cast a jaundiced eye on this charade and fans reassured one another with reminders that Adams had spent his entire adult life in their midst and would never seriously consider leaving.

With Herzeg pulling strings behind the scenes, however, and Astros owner John J. McMullen, who held the lease on the Astrodome, quietly lending support, enough pressure was brought to bear to secure what Herzeg really wanted. In 1988, Harris County, which owns the Astrodome, spent $67 million of public money on renovations, much of it to build 66 luxury boxes and add 8,500 seats, the tribute Herzeg had demanded for Adams to keep the team in town. For area sports fans, the emotional cost was the loss of the original scoreboard, which exploded into a Wild West panorama including a snorting bull and a cowboy twirling a lasso every time an Astro hit a home run or an Oiler scored. Adams signed a 10-year lease extension, to run through the 1997 season.

When Adams and Herzeg finally parted ways over a squabble over money — Herzeg was making $450,000 a year and wanted a hefty raise on his new contract — the owner brought back Mike McClure, this time as chief confidant and espionage agent. McClure had left the organization when he found his way to the boss's ear blocked by Herzeg, who was difficult to circumnavigate, and taken a marketing job with the Chicago White Sox. Eager to make his mark, McClure soon told Adams that Herzeg had done a lousy job of wringing concessions on the Astrodome renovation and that he could secure a better deal. When he contacted the Houston Sports Association, the McMullen-controlled company that held the lease, he received a reply best characterized as rude, and left at that.

McClure then set out to get the great man a great new stadium in Houston. The concept he cooked up involved a downtown dome for football and basketball. McClure priced it — conservatively, some thought — at $240 million. An architectural firm he retained built a model that brought to mind the world's biggest doll house. Barbie might have loved this pad, but no one else did. With the community evincing no enthusiasm, McClure invited media members individually to his office in the Adams Petroleum Company building to show off his toy, complete with moving walls and grandstands sliding on rails to change configurations. A kid with his first erector set couldn't have been prouder.

But McClure might as well have been playing Dungeons and Dragons.

His brainchild simmered with no outright rejections, on the record, anyway, from public officials while everyone awaited a response from the Rockets. Owner Leslie Alexander took his time, but when he finally spoke he said the Oilers had concocted the scheme without consulting him and that he had no interest in moving his team into a dome. That torpedo sent the Bud Dome to the bottom belching bubbles. McClure had known all along that he could never sell such an expenditure for a football-only facility that would be used by Adams's team on about 10 dates a year and compete with the county-owned Astrodome for conventions and other events.

Perhaps today, McClure still has his model and uses it to stage those miniature electric football games that were popular in the '50s.

And maybe neither he nor Adams was terribly upset when the Bud Dome sank. Various interests in Houston floated alternative ideas, a new open-air arena, a refurbished Rice Stadium with luxury suites added to its 72,000-seat capacity, another renovation and update of the Astrodome. Adams said no, no, and no. He would consider a new stadium with a roof designed for football or nothing at all. Music City had begun crooning in his ear. McClure was practically screaming into it to begin packing now, but then he had a more com-pelling motive than doing the by-durn best job he could for his boss.

In Houston, the one irrefutable argument in favor of caving in to Adams turned on the experience of other cities that had lost teams. In each case — notably those of St. Louis and Baltimore — getting a replacement franchise took a decade or longer and cost far more than the outlay required to keep the old club. With more than $50 million still owed on the $67 million investment in the Astrodome about seven years earlier, however, taxpayers were not inclined toward any more gifts for Bud, except perhaps a banjo to take to Tennessee. Bob Lanier, the mayor, said he sounded out prominent members of the business community and found not one willing to throw his weight behind a campaign to raise private funding for a new football stadium.

Public-opinion polling by the *Houston Chronicle* in August, 1995, indicated a similar response from ordinary citizens. Asked for their reaction to spending public funds to keep the Oilers in Houston, pro-viding that no increase in sales or property tax be used, thirty percent of respondents were in favor, fifty-eight percent opposed. On the matter of using public money to attract another NFL franchise under the same stipulations should the Oilers leave, forty-one percent were in favor, forty-one percent opposed.

By the end of the year, with the threat of the team's departure now very real, attitudes softened but opponents of public funds to keep the Oilers still outnumbered advocates by forty-nine percent to thirty-seven percent even though football ranked slightly ahead of basketball as the favorite pro sport in the city. Six months after the Rockets won their second consecutive NBA championship, Alexander received a favorable opinion from sixty-eight percent of those polled, to sixty-one percent for Astros owner Drayton McLane, Jr., to seven percent for Adams.

Bud's personal popularity, understandably, had reached its nadir as he plotted to pull his team out of the city, but he had never been Houston's favorite pin-up. He wasn't revered even in the early days, but whatever esteem he once enjoyed was eroded by the firing of the hugely popular Bum Phillips after the 1980 season and the strong-arm tactics he employed to bring about the Astrodome renovation, to say nothing of Herzeg's antics. Despite the prevailing sentiment toward the owner and the team's failures on the field, however, Houston had poured millions into Adams's pockets. When McClure was campaigning for a new stadium in Houston, he repeatedly cited that the team had consistently performed before crowds of more than 100 percent of Astrodome capacity. Only when the Oilers were putting up a 2-14 record as Adams was batting his eyelashes at Nashville did attendance begin to slide.

Still, Bud told his fellow owners he needed to flee Houston because of the city's failure to support his club. They agreed, in the belief, no doubt, that suckers deserve a sucker punch.

"I know there has to be more behind it than money," said Bum Phillips. "You don't take the Oilers out of a great town like Houston just for money." Maybe he was right.

If the club's 37 seasons were replayed from start to finish like a festival of Alfred Hitchcock films, Adams would be Hitchcock, remaining in the background until he emerged from the shadows for a cameo, and then as suddenly dissolving until the mood for another walk-on overtook him. At times, he appeared fascinated with his toy; at others, completely disinterested.

Never has he taken a role like that assumed by some of the new-breed owners such as Jerry Jones of Dallas and Edward DeBartolo, Jr., of San Francisco, who bounce along the sideline dealing hugs and high-fives like bags of gum drops. On the other hand, neither does he demonstrate the quiet grace of the late Art Rooney of Pittsburgh or Adams's AFL co-founder, Lamar Hunt of Kansas City. Throughout his life in football, Bud has always seemed to be caught in between, unable to decide if he wanted to be involved or aloof, on the point or bringing up the rear. In some seasons, he has traveled with his team frequently; in others, hardly at all.

For home games, Adams has opened his home to friends and taken them by bus to the Astrodome, where he entertained in his press-level suite. Occasionally, the television cameras would catch him looking chipper, a glass of Jack Daniels-and-Coke in hand, and he would shimmy into a life-of-the-party jig — or was it the Watusi? For Jones, the hell-raiser with a limo full of party girls in tow, the gesture would come off as spontaneous. Adams wore it like a cockamamie hat and food-spotted tie on New Year's Eve, a man wishing he knew how to cut loose and have a good time. A psychiatrist watching on TV might have wondered if this was a boy in his early 70s, still trying to choose the right reaction for a father who would never be pleased.

Bud's public-relations instincts easily matched those of Spiro Agnew and George Steinbrenner. He kept himself quarantined from fans, instructing stadium security to meet his bus on arrival and whisk him and his guests to his private box with such vigor that no contact with the public was possible, save for the impromptu hecklers who happened to spy him on his way in and fire off a few choice words after his negotiations with Nashville became public. In his rare appearances before the media, he often fumbled thoughts and then gushed words so improbable they generated embarrassed laughter, as when he said he had ordered coach Jack Pardee to wear a headset. "I don't care whether it's turned on or not," Adams said. "I just think it

looks better if he has a headset on." On other occasions, he put on a
diffident grin as though to say he enjoyed watching the pot boil. Ladd
Herzeg gave him many opportunities to perfect this routine.

But Adams's handlers kept him shielded from inquiring minds
most of the time. One-on-one interviews were limited to a very select
few known to pander to well-known individuals interested in ventur-
ing only into areas of their own choosing. Keeping a multi-millionaire
on his leash twenty-four hours a day, however, remains as daunting a
challenge as it sounds.

Bud broke free long enough to call a sports talk show on the
Oilers' flagship station after hearing himself come under attack from
the co-hosts as well as callers. His dalliance with Nashville was in the
heavy-breathing stage and talkers were sizzling. "You know, if they
don't want us here, I accept that," Adams said. "We're going to leave,
and you helped us leave. I'm not criticizing y'all. You have to look
after yourself. We have to look after ourselves. We would like to stay
here, don't get me wrong. I'd love to stay here in Houston. It's not in
the cards. You've said, 'Get rid of Bud.' Well, we're going to leave."
Several times, he expressed wonder at the portrayal of him as a villain.
"Everyone hates Bud," he said. "I have heard that before on the program. Why does everyone hate Bud? What have I done?"

Maybe it wasn't all about money. Maybe it was about love.

2

IN THE
BEGINNING

The 1978 football season, and as Texans we know that season begins January 1 and runs through December 31, has certainly been one of great excitement for thousands of Houston Oiler fans throughout the state and for those Houston Oiler fans throughout the nation.

The packed stadium, the pompons, the fight song, the huge radio network carrying our games to a vast audience, the crowds that greet the team upon its arrival from the road games, and the excitement of the fan on the streets has certainly been a great thrill.

After V-J Day while still in the U.S. Navy Air Corps, I stopped in Houston for several days because of bad weather. After that visit I made up my mind that Houston was the city where I wanted to make my home. I have never regretted that decision.

Our city today is the focal point of the world. We have a clean city, a city people want to move to and raise their families, a city that is getting *bigger and better every day.*

And now, even more attention has been directed to Houston because of the Houston Oilers. The Oilers are not "just another pro football team." It's a team with a personality that everyone in America can relate to. We have a host of young people, some veteran players, a group that plays together, and a team that forgets about its injuries and hurts, and defies the odds that are against it every week. They just go out and win.

The City of Houston told the world, "This is our team" and I am proud that the recognition has come, not only to the football team, recognition that they so richly deserve, but also to the people of the city. We are proud as an organization that we have been able to build the club to the point that they have now achieved.

Even though we weren't the victors Sunday, I firmly believe that we have put together for the City of Houston a team it can be rightly proud of, and a team that will be in the forefront of the National Football League for many years to come.

There are those who will say that having a sports franchise is not important to the city, nor is the success of a sports franchise important to a city. I know better. Look at the personal pride the people in Cincinnati have developed for the Reds, or the immense following and recognition that the Packers have brought to Green Bay, even what the Kentucky Derby means to Louisville and the "500" means to Indianapolis.

When we play at home, thousands of men and women and young people have jobs on Sunday, or to earn overtime, simply because the Oilers are playing. It is a fact that because of the home Oiler games extra bus drivers, extra cab drivers, cooks, waiters and waitresses, bus boys, concession salespeople, traffic policemen and so forth take home something extra in their paychecks, and when people have some extra money, they in turn will spend that money on products and services, and that in turn provides a better income and a way of life for others.

Our players have given untold hours of their time to work with local charities and fund-raising projects and because of their presence, these events are more likely to succeed. The football team has given the young people of our community something to look up to, and something to get involved with. Anything that provides our youth with something whole-some has to be good for the whole community.

Even though the Oilers aren't making plans this day for Miami and Super Bowl XIII, we'll be there next year.

I appreciate this opportunity to say thank you on behalf of the players, coaches, and entire organization for the great support you gave the Houston Oilers this past season.

— Bud Adams, in a *Houston Chronicle* guest column, January 8, 1979

Kenneth Stanley Adams earned the nickname "Boots" in the devastating Kansas City flood of 1907. Safely billeted on high ground, the eight-year-old son of a railroad engineer pulled on a pair of bright red waders and sloshed into the flooded area to help victims to safety and invited them into his family's home.

At Kansas University, he played football and basketball, spending one summer in Bartlesville, Oklahoma, hauling ice to get in shape. When he married after his junior year, he took a job in the Oklahoma company town with Phillips 66 as a warehouse clerk. In 1921, he organized an after-work basketball team known as the "66 Oilers," which later sent star players to Olympics teams. At age thirty-eight, he became president of Phillips, and thereupon he almost died.

On a trip to Chicago, Boots Adams and two employees ate contaminated food and contracted amoebic dysentery. Back in Bartlesville, his two companions died and Adams, clinging to life, asked to be flown to Kansas City to end his days in his boyhood home. A physician there, experimenting with a cure for the deadly disease, scored a breakthrough in his treatment of Adams, who would retire as Phillips president at sixty-five. The $200 million company he had joined as a clerk was by then worth $1.8 billion.

He stayed on as chairman of the board and of the finance committee, and when he turned sixty-six, Bartlesville had all the symbolism it needed to throw a wing-ding fit for a musical. Dwight D. Eisenhower, the seventy-four-year-old former president, was among the thousands who turned out to honor Boots in a day-long rain. The company threw the party and the town changed its name to "Bootsville" for the day. Under Boots's leadership, Phillips 66 had bought up so many leases in the Oklahoma panhandle that it became one of the world's largest natural-gas producers and the state's largest corporation.

As company towns go, the Bartlesville of Bud Adams's youth was a benevolent place, and a sports-minded one. Of the company's 7,000 employees, seven in eight participated in swimming, basketball, or track at the athletic facility at the headquarters complex. The philosopher Eric Hoffer found something to like in Phillips because its employees "look like they haven't been run over by life."

Nor was the son of the chairman. After stops at Culver Military Academy in Indiana and Menlo College in California, Bud Adams followed his father to Kansas University, where he, too, played football and basketball. The Culver yearbook awarded him the ultimate accolade, "a lad that few girls could resist"; his college newspaper described a "slim-hipped" sophomore halfback with "dazzling speed."

He studied petroleum engineering at Kansas and met his wife, Nancy, who lived in the sorority house next door on Greek Row, joined the Navy toward the end of World War II and took training in aeronautical engineering at Notre Dame. After a year in the Pacific as an engineering officer, he was discharged as a lieutenant. On his way to New Orleans to see the Sugar Bowl, he was grounded in Houston by fog in 1945, took a look around and decided to stay.

While many of his decisions in running the Oilers appear to have been made in a fog as well, Bud's horizons were clear as he launched his business career. Boots helped. In interviews over the years, Bud has mentioned Boots only in the context of maintaining an identity separate from his father's. "I decided early on I would never be tied to his suspenders, nor to his company," he said. "I am not."

Some said Boots, like other mahatmas of his generation, maintained two families, and that Bud came from the one he favored less. One thing dad and lad did not share was an appetite for physical labor. On a summer vacation from college, Bud reported for duty on a painting crew working on Phillips 66 properties. The foreman waited until his father visited the site to fire him.

"Mr. Adams," the man said, "Bud don't want to work and I got boys sittin' over there with families to feed who cain't get work. I cain't keep him on while their families go hungry."

"You're right," Boots said with a nod, and he drove away.

After the Navy, Bud did get a boost from Boots, but he was always vague as to its extent. He said he arrived in Houston with $18,000 in savings and "some stock my father had given me." At various times, he pegged the value of the stock at $10,000 and $100,000. Whatever the figure, it was probably of less value than the exclusive franchise he received from Phillips 66 as distributor for the Texas Gulf Coast.

Bud opened his first station in Houston in 1946 and by the end of the year he was operating twelve outlets. From distribution, he segued into exploration and production. Three early wells in 1947 produced a modest yield of twenty to twenty-five barrels a day. Over the next twelve years, he estimated, his Ada Resources drilled about a thousand wells. Bud said he went in search of oil in the ground for "the romance of being an oilman, to call myself an oilman instead of a pump jockey."

His business interests diversified, and in 1959 Bud Adams graduated into the Foolish Club. Membership consisted of the eight original owners of American Football League franchises, brash enough to take on the entrenched NFL, strong enough to endure the bleeding of the early years, and lucky enough to be folded into the older league when Congress exempted pro football from antitrust laws to allow a merger. It didn't hurt, either, that a fellow named Joe Namath came along.

Adams had been in pursuit of an NFL franchise for some time, coming closest to buying the Chicago Cardinals in November, 1958. He met with the Bidwill family, which owned that club, in Florida and learned that he would be allowed to move the franchise to Houston - but only to buy 49 per cent. Without control, he wasn't interested. Four months later, Lamar Hunt showed up on his doorstep.

Ever since, Adams has been credited as co-founder of the AFL, and accurately so, but the new league was Hunt's brainchild. An heir to a Dallas oil fortune, Hunt flew into Houston and went to dinner with Adams. "We finished eating," Adams would later recall, "and he finally asked me if I would be interested in having a football team in a new league. I said, 'Hell, yes.'"

The NFL soon learned of their plotting. In July of 1959, the co-conspirators were summoned to Chicago for a clandestine meeting with George Halas. The Bears owner promised that if they would abandon their plan he would assure each an NFL franchise. He did not, however, say when. In Houston a few days later, Hunt and Adams announced the birth of the AFL. By the fall, franchises had been awarded to Houston, Dallas, Buffalo, Denver, Oakland, Los Angeles, New York, and Boston. The sanity of each owner was called into question more than once.

Ralph Wilson lived in Detroit and wanted a team in Miami, where he maintained a second home, but couldn't secure a lease on the Orange Bowl. He settled for Buffalo, a city he had never visited. "My friends thought I was a real chump," Wilson said later. "I live in Detroit, so to those guys it was like trying to challenge General Motors or Ford. Guys wouldn't drink with me at the bar. They would go stand in a corner and not speak to me. They all laughed at me."

In Houston, Adams encountered a similar reaction. "To the guys on the street, it was a real gamble," he said. "I was going to sell some interest in the team but I couldn't get anybody to take it."

In November, the league conducted its first draft of college players in Minneapolis, which was to have had a charter franchise until the NFL, in one last bid to sabotage the upstarts, awarded that city an expansion club. Halas also offered Adams a team for $650,000. "I told him I had given Lamar Hunt my word back in July and I was going to stick to it," he said.

Oakland replaced Minneapolis, and Houston made Billy Cannon, the 1959 Heisman Trophy winner from Louisiana State University, its first draft choice. Pete Rozelle, general manager of the Los Angeles Rams of the NFL, also drafted Cannon. The Oilers won a court battle and signed him for $30,000. So began a franchise that called

Jeppesen Stadium, a rickety structure on the University of Houston campus, its home.

Many other wars over players followed, some landing in court. After reeling in Cannon, the Oilers lost most of their other bouts with the NFL, which signed such Houston draftees as Oklahoma tackle Ralph Neely and Texas linebacker Tommy Nobis. Neely signed after the final regular-season game of his college career in 1965 in violation of National Collegiate Athletic Association rules to save $8,000 in federal income tax. When Adams disclosed the contract on television, apparently to scare NFL teams away from his prized recruit, Neely was ruled ineligible for Oklahoma's Gator Bowl game with Florida State.

"Adams went back on his word," said a seething Neely, who then signed with the Dallas Cowboys and went on to a distinguished career in the NFL. An accounting and finance major in college, he said he would have forgone professional football rather than play for the Oilers if they had prevailed in court. "I would have gone into banking or something," he said.

The Oilers got the jump on their AFL rivals and won the first two championships. In 1961, the league's second season, George Blanda threw thirty-six touchdown passes in fourteen games. Charlie Hennigan and Bill Groman cradled most of Blanda's throws, Cannon carried the ball, and such worthies as Hogan Wharton and Bob Talamini knocked open the holes he ran through. The Oilers beat the Chargers, who played in Los Angeles for one season and then moved to San Diego, for those first two titles. In 1962, they posted their best regular-season record, 11-3, but lost to Hunt's Dallas Texans in the championship game.

Many of the other clubs were slower to assemble talent. "I didn't have many good players that first year," Wilson said of his Buffalo team. "It was like a squad of bartenders and school teachers."

In Houston, artistic growth outstripped financial. Like many other start-up businesses, the Oilers lost money, $445,000 in 1960 and $418,000 in the second season. The fledgling league's first television contract paid each team $185,000 in the inaugural season, but ratings didn't reach the anticipated level and that number dropped to $125,000 for 1961. The all-conquering Oilers were pulling in fans as though each man were equipped with a magic flute, however, and offset that $60,000 hickey with swelling crowds. The first-year top attendance of 25,247 was eclipsed four times in 1961, and two crowds numbered more than 35,000.

The brawling young league was cutting teeth at a predictably painful rate, and Adams's fights with the NFL soon seemed tepid compared to his feuds on the local scene. Even in the most successful years the franchise would ever know on a Houston field, Bud didn't employ coaches so much as rent them. Lou Rymkus master-minded that first championship season, but he was replaced in 1961 by Wally Lemm. The team won another title, but Lemm gave way in 1962 to Frank "Pop" Ivy.

Despite the loss in the championship game, Ivy returned the next season — and the team hit the skids. Beginning in 1963, the Oilers compiled records of 6-8 under Ivy, 4-10 under Sammy Baugh, 4-10 under Hugh "Bones" Taylor and 3-11 under the reincarnated Lemm. By the time Lemm returned the Oilers to respectability on the field in 1967 with a 9-4-1 record and an Eastern Division title, Adams should have required his head coaches to wear numbers on their backs as the players did.

One interested observer of this chaos was a fellow who spurned a job offer from Adams in the beginning to coach the NFL entry in

Dallas, a team that forced Hunt's Texans to beat a hasty retreat to Kansas City, where they became the Chiefs. In 1984, entering the Cowboys' twenty-fifth season, Tom Landry looked back on the five Super Bowls in which his team had played and decided he had chosen well. "I can remember Bud Adams wanting to bring me to the Houston Oilers," he said. "I think I made the best choice. I would have been one of fifty coaches there."

As usual in pro sports, an owner's ability to put a good product on the field had less to do with profitability than market forces with a mind of their own. Through all the hits and misses of the first four years, the per-team slice of the television pie dropped to $100,000. In 1964, NBC-TV decided against all odds that the AFL had arrived, more than anything else because it needed sports programming, and negotiated a deal that paid each franchise $900,000 annually.

That contract caught the NFL upside the head like a forearm shiver, and the merger became a simple matter of working out details. Ralph Wilson dickered over those with Carroll Rosenbloom, owner of the Los Angeles Rams of the NFL, in a series of meetings in Miami in 1965. The merger was announced in 1966, and might have come sooner if not for several AFL big cigars who wanted to play hardball. Adams was one of those feeling the testosterone rush.

"It was starting to be a bloody mess for the NFL," he said, referring to player salaries streaking into the high six figures as the leagues waged bidding wars for talent. "By then, we had good crowds and I couldn't see any downside to it. The league was going to make it. If anything, I felt we merged with the NFL too soon."

Adams got shanghaied into the best deal of his life. Elsewhere, AFL attendance was building but the coach-a-year Oilers were retreating at the gate and doing nothing to enhance the value of the television package. AFL owners bought into the established league for $2 million each, with ten equal annual installments at zero interest. The melding of the leagues for scheduling and playoff purposes didn't take place until 1970 but the combined draft began in 1967, ending the blood-letting and bringing players' salaries under control. From that day on, life might have been all sunshine and daffodils. In Bud's case, of course, it was one hangover after another.

3

SHAKING THE MONEY TREE

The exemption from antitrust laws Congress granted to allow the football merger put everyone with a stake in a pro franchise on Easy Street. Combined with the explosive growth in the game's popularity, it insulated every owner against his own stupidity, no matter how vast. A 10-year-old with a learning disability could operate a club profitably if he could turn on the lights.

Over the years since 1966, television networks have executed a succession of contracts that would have gone down as felony bungling if done in another industry. Often, the justification has been promoting the programs that would follow the football telecast. But perhaps of greater weight has been TV executives' desire to rub elbows with team owners at Super Bowl parties — sometimes without spilling their martinis — and collect autographs from star players for their kids.

Franchise free agency for fun and profit (of which more later) has evolved to the point that American cities are nothing more than slots on the owners' roulette wheel. Fans do the gambling — billions are bet on pro football each year by citizen/fans who quibble tirelessly over spending relative shekels of tax dollars on new stadiums, to say nothing of new schools — while team owners rake off the profits like casino operators.

A rooting interest in a team that blows town can be replaced on a weekly basis by whatever squad that happens to be getting the right number on the line. There's nothing like a C-note or a grand on the nose to make a fan-atic of anybody with access to a TV and a six-pack on Sunday afternoon. Or Sunday night, or Monday night, or Thursday night, or Saturday after the college season. Even the Christians can look good against the Lions if you get 16 1/2 and an over-under of 31.

The NFL has worked up a wonderful comic opera in which it takes a scowling stance against gambling on its games, even to the point of flying in lawyers with briefcases full of stern admonitions when a state conceives a lottery game based on football scores. The league keeps a private cop in each city — in addition to the team's own security apparatus — to watch out for players who might associate with serious gamblers, as well as drug dealers.

It's little wonder the brass cultivates an image of purity, at least outside of Dallas. If the investing public ever began to question whether players were on the take to throw games, the product would be flattened like a quarterback drilled in the back by a raging defensive end.

Whether Bud Adams's team plays in Texas or Tennessee, the bookies will make a line and fans will get down, and they will watch. Advertisers will buy. Mammon will be in his heaven, and capitalism will be safe.

The owner's job is finding a way to maximize his profit after paying his players enough so that they won't be seriously tempted by shady characters who would fix games. He also must put a competitive team on the field, but the Oilers' experience in Houston suggests that fans are generous in their definition of "competitive." After almost four decades of futility, customers were still able to get their juices flowing over a new quarterback drafted in the first round or the promise engendered by a first-round flop in the playoffs the season before.

This is an industry in which the businessman faces no competition and no imperative to create demand for his product. The market is self-stimulating, and any gaps are filled by a fawning sports media that provide gratis exposure for which other enterprises pay millions. Even when they're ripping the overpaid running back or the cocaine-snorting cornerback, they're focusing attention on the Nasties, who might just "overcome adversity" this year and go all the way. Players with rap sheets longer than their lists of college credits make wonderful fodder for coaches who love nothing better than talking about overcoming adversity, without regard to that which is self-inflicted.

Should the owner find his profits slipping, he simply turns to the tried-and-true expedient of extorting more money from his community, or another one. If NFL owners ever get serious about adding some color to their meetings, they should consider the sleazy boxing promoter Don King, who comes equipped with a slogan that fits quite nicely: "Only in America."

Long before the practice and the buzz phrase "franchise free agency" came into vogue, Bud Adams knew something about leverage. He began complaining about unacceptable financial losses and snarling like a baboon about moving his team or selling it to interests in another city shortly after he opened the doors. Every time Mickey Rooney dumped another wife, it seemed, Bud threatened to divorce Houston.

Just as Lamar Hunt had handed him the AFL and the Oilers, Judge Roy Hofheinz served up the Astrodome. The original owner of the Houston Astros, Hofheinz conceived a covered stadium for a climate as thick with mosquitoes as with humidity in summertime. Moving into the first dome — the Eighth Wonder of the World, as it was dubbed — proved as laborious for Adams, however, as giving birth to it had for Hofheinz, his former business partner.

How these boys did feud. Protracted negotiations that played out in public hit a high point when Bud growled, "Any NFL owner who agrees that the Dome is the Eighth Wonder of the World will also have to admit that Roy Hofheinz's contract terms are the Ninth Wonder." Voters in Nashville, told over and over by Adams while he was dickering with their city dads that he is a man of his word, might have been amused to learn of Hofheinz's account of his dealings with Adams in the mid-'60s. Or perhaps not.

"What hurt me most," Hofheinz said, "was that Bud and I met one week before he announced he was going to Rice (Stadium). He pumped my hand and slapped me on the back and told me it was a deal. We were supposed to meet the next Monday and put the whole thing in writing. We called on Monday and the Oiler executives were busy. We called again on Wednesday and they were still busy.

"I wasn't worried because we had a deal. The next Friday, my secretary got a call at 1:11 p.m. The Oilers told her quite succinctly that they were going to sign with Rice at 1:15 p.m. I had already left Houston. She caught me during a stop in Montreal and told me."

The Oilers had earlier announced an agreement to move into the Astrodome and a hike in ticket prices necessitated by higher rent.

When the deal collapsed and they landed in the more affordable Rice Stadium, they did not rescind the increase.

Adams claimed Hofheinz had dealt in bad faith and later said he would have moved the club if he hadn't reached agreement with Rice University for his team to play in its stadium. "If Rice hadn't made its stadium available, I would have been faced with one of two decisions. I could either have sold the team or moved it. Nobody in his right mind is getting out of pro football these days, so I imagine that I would have been forced to shift the franchise."

At the top of his list was Atlanta. "They're ready for pro football, they have the [stadium] and I'm sure I could have received a break on the rent. There are at least five other cities that I would have considered, Philadelphia, Cleveland, Chicago, Anaheim, and New Orleans."

In 1965, Adams signed a five-year lease with Rice. By 1967, he was complaining of poor attendance and losses he projected at $300,000 for the season. "Let's be honest about this," he said. "Seattle is going to get a pro football team. There probably isn't going to be another expansion franchise granted until after the American and National Leagues complete their merger in 1970. So somebody is going to grab off that rich market. If Seattle came to me with an outstanding deal, I'd be a fool to turn it down." He had, he said, spoken with people in Seattle about moving his team.

Years later, he said he had considered a move to Seattle more seriously than any other he had ever contemplated. "Seattle was talking about building a big stadium . . . and they approached me about moving my team. They had no pro football in the Northwest and they wanted a team badly. We were about ready to sit down and talk seriously, but a campaign was started in Houston — 'Let's save the Oilers' — and we dropped it."

By 1968, Adams had a deal with Hofheinz to play in the Astrodome. Rice University officials, still operating under a contract with two years remaining for the Oilers to play in their stadium, learned of his agreement with Hofheinz through press accounts. Rice elected not to pursue legal remedies. Adams said, "Much has been made of a so-called feud between Judge Hofheinz and me. I would be remiss if I did not dispel such rumors, for they are exactly that, rumors. We are both businessmen and naturally seek the best terms we each can obtain."

Negotiations had gone on longer than the Paris peace talks, but then cash was at stake, not mere lives.

The Oilers would remain in the Astrodome as long as they would remain in Houston, and Adams would continue to gripe about his status as a tenant in a building controlled by the local baseball owner. By 1975, he was arguing for more seats funded with tax dollars and, perhaps not coincidentally, talking about selling the franchise again. "If we can get together on price," he said of his negotiations with a group of investors, "some sort of sale will be made." While some of the investors were out-of-towners, Bud said it was his intent that the team remain in Houston.

Less than a month later, he had experienced a change of heart, if such a thing was anatomically possible. A stirring 13-10 victory by the Oilers over the Washington Redskins was the stimulus. "I'm not saying I won't sell if somebody walks through the door with a good offer," he said, "but I'm not looking for buyers now. It was an emotional time for me when I said that. There was talk about the players going on strike, but several players have come to me recently and told me they wanted me to keep the club."

He didn't identify the players.

Through it all, Adams sparred with many people he couldn't fire and some he did. Even Battlin' Al Davis was pressed into duty as referee in one of Bud's bouts. At an AFL executive committee meeting in Houston at which he took office as the league's commissioner, Davis discovered his first duty was breaking up a fracas between Adams and Jack Gallagher, a veteran sports reporter with the *Houston Post*.

Gallagher and a photographer were lining up a picture of Davis and other league officials when an argument developed between Adams and Gallagher over who would be in the picture. A scuffle ensued, and Davis and some owners separated the two, probably much to the relief of Gallagher, who was not in Bud's weight class. Adams later said the fight erupted as the result of "something that had been brewing for over six years."

Very little good was brewed on the field. The Oilers finished the 1973 season with a 1-13 record and a four-season record of 9-45-2. The players had worked for four head coaches in four years, and another change was anticipated. Sid Gillman, the general manager, had replaced Bill Peterson as coach but didn't plan to continue in the job because of health problems. Adams cited a lack of continuity as the primary reason for the reign of error but pronounced Gillman an improvement over his predecessor. "Pete was right out of college," he said. "All of it was new to him. I prefer it the way we have it now with Sid running the show. Whatever's done is done right."

Even in those early years, Adams couldn't settle on a style for running his organization. As would become clear to the public later, the figure with the greatest say was usually a bean-counter, and the one point on which the owner was adamant was that no football man ever consolidate power. Later would come annual contract hassles with top draft picks that kept key players out of summer camp so long that their value to the team was diminished because they missed valuable on-the-job training. Adams was embarrassed in the 1980s — in this rare instance he lashed out at the messenger — when it was reported that his front-office staff had gone three years without raises. And the training facility was only replaced years after it had become worse than an eyesore, with players complaining of furry creatures that shared their quarters and toilets that broke down so often that at times only one was available to more than 50 men.

In these instances, it was never clear whether the boss was just plain cheap or was out to show the football people who was boss.

Peterson found the situation intolerable, and probably sealed his fate in a memo he wrote to Adams following a 1-13 season in 1972. Among his points:

- "There is a pressing need for the Head Coach to be able to make decisions on a day-to-day basis that effect (sic) his program . . . Often, on the slightest matter, I must waste a day seeking out someone in authority."
- "Often our press conferences give appearance of either internal conflict, or lack of preparation."
- "There is a very unhealthy dichotomy of thinking around the Oiler Organization.
  a) The attitude that there are Bill Peterson people and Bud Adams people.
  b) For instance, it appears that only the coaching staff is loyal to the Head Coach.
  c) The rest of the staff was 'here before this coach came and maybe here when he is gone.'

d) This is unhealthy. Why should the Head Coach have to compete
   with the owner of the Oilers for loyalty? This is like one man paying two people not to get along with each other . . ."

• "I have heard — even from within the organization — that it is not
  important for the Oilers to be one of the top teams, but rather to
  play respectable football."

• "Bud Adams needs a winner. After so many years and so many
  players and so many coaches, the public will, in time, come to a
  point of holding the owner solely responsible for a consistent loser.
  The owner is not expected to be a coach, but he is expected to provide the things necessary to build a winner. A losing team, in time,
  will reflect on the owner."

On the last count, whether on all the others or not, Peterson was
unquestionably right. Five games into the next season, all losses, he
was fired.

Gillman finished out that 1973 season as coach and came back to
post a 7-7 record the next year. It was the Oilers' best record since '68,
but his employer was not pleased. Gillman had exceeded the 47-man
roster limit in '73, and the league had fined the team $15,000. "I
made it understood that if there were any fines like that this year, it
was going to come out of somebody else's pocket," said Adams, who
complained of losing $459,000 after saying during the season he
would break even on the year.

"We set a budget again this year, too. It embarrasses me to be the
owner of the only club losing money in the NFL. It makes me look
like a poor owner, and I don't want to be the laughingstock of the
owners around the league. If I spent as much as Sid wants me to
spend, I'd be the winningest owner — but I'd also be the brokest."

Two months after that remarkable turnaround season, Gillman

was gone. "If I could have gotten the controls I wanted, I'd still be coaching," he said. "I thought it over and decided this would be best for everyone. Bud doesn't need a general manager. He wants to run his own ballclub. I don't want to go out in a wave of name-calling. It was interesting, in some ways a beautiful year in Houston. I thought when I got there, I still think, it could be a fabulous franchise."

Twenty years and zero trips to the Super Bowl later, so did many people in Tennessee.

4

SAVIOR IN A STETSON

A thin smile flickered across John Breen's lips as he looked down on the Oilers' pregame drills from the press box. "Carl Mauck," said the Oilers' former general manager. "He hasn't blocked anybody in a year and a half, but there he is, still the center, still the starter."

As a blocker, Mauck made a pretty lousy singer, but nobody cared about his skills in that area, either. He recorded a lilting piece of doggerel titled "The Oiler Cannonball," sung to the tune of "The Wabash Cannonball." For a year, it seemed you couldn't turn on the radio in Houston without hearing Mauck croaking:

From the fancy-passin' Dago
To the Tyler bowling ball

Other light classics filled the airwaves as well in the late '70s. Wide receiver Kenny Burrough, more consistent as a singer than he was at holding the ball on routes over the middle, recorded "The Super Bowl Itch." Their deficiencies on the field or in the studio didn't matter. They were Bum's boys, and Bum and his boys owned Houston.

In restaurants, they would have had to level machine guns and take every last soul hostage to pay for a meal. Or a drink, and they did drink. The fancy-passin' Dago was quarterback Dan Pastorini; the Tyler bowling ball was Earl Campbell, the best back to hit the NFL since Jim Brown. Leon Gray and Bob Young anchored the line and Curley Culp and Robert Brazile led a defense that stuck everything that moved. Houston couldn't have loved these guys more if they'd been named Bradshaw, Harris, Swann, Greene, Ham, and Lambert. And they loved Bum.

Other pro football coaches have commanded as much respect but none as much loyalty as Oail Andrew "Bum" Phillips. With his players, he had the touch of a trainer patting a colt's flank, and they ran for him until they dropped. Kenny Stabler, the Alabama redneck, read the game plan by the light of the juke box, and Gifford Nielsen, the milkshake-drinking Mormon from Brigham Young University, wouldn't say "heck" if the word was in the name of a play. As Bum might have said, and probably did, "Don't matter none. They all good bo-oys."

Terry Bradshaw, the rawboned kid from Louisiana who played quarterback for the Steelers, beat the Oilers in the playoffs like urchins right out of a Dickensian orphanage, then regaled anyone who would listen of his love for Bum.

The first time, the players had no idea of what to expect. They had lost to the Steelers in Pittsburgh, 34-5, in the American Conference championship game and their flight home had been delayed by weather. They knew they were the first Houston team ever even to play for the AFC title, that their 10-6 season and two playoff victories had electrified the city, and that a radio station-sponsored pep rally in the Astrodome awaited their return, win or lose.

They also knew the Steelers had just handed them their headgear without removing their heads. As they approached the stadium in three buses, they pressed noses to the windows and peered out at a parking lot jammed with thousands of cars. Some speculated the boat show at the Astrohall next door must have drawn a whopping crowd. "After we lost," said linebacker Gregg Bingham, "I thought there'd only be a few people sweeping up the place."

The buses pulled up to the ramp at a service entrance in center field and stopped. A police officer boarded each bus in turn and warned the party that, once inside, it was every man for himself. He cautioned them that delirious fans might come cascading out of the stands and onto the floor and advised in that eventuality that they take refuge back in the buses. With that admonition haunting their thoughts, the gate rose and they pulled forward out of the darkness and onto the set of Blazing Saddles.

Forty-five thousand fans, many of whom had waited more than four hours, set up a din that swallowed the blaring music of an amplified band. The players blinked through blazing lights and into a sea of adoring faces. Defensive end Andy Dorris, still seated on a bus, wondered, "Can you imagine what would have happened if we'd won?"

Players climbed onto a stage — fans remained under control in their frenzy — and addressed the crowd. When his turn came, Pastorini hung back for a moment to gather his composure. "We'll bust our butts to try to win Super Bowl XIV for you next year," he said, and he could say no more.

"We lost the game," said Phillips, "but with this kind of support, we're not losers."

Mike Barber, a tight end who never liked to be tackled, had suffered a knee injury in the game. A cowboy hat topping his flowing hair and woolly beard, he raised his metal crutches to the high ceiling with head bowed like a crippled Rocky trying to take flight, and the roar almost blew the roof to Pittsburgh.

When the buses transported them to a far corner of the parking lot where they had left their cars, fans thronged their path, banging on the buses and yelling, "We're No. 1" . . .

The second time, it got wild.

Fifty-five thousand fans waited as long as five and a half hours to greet the team on its return from a 27-13 loss in Pittsburgh. Another 15,000 to 20,000 were turned away at the gates, and still more lined the route from the airport to the stadium to sing their hosannas to Bum's battered bruisers. When the building filled and the gates were sealed before the team's arrival, thousands of fans tore down three gates and a section of fence and streamed into the parking lot. Police arrested those they could catch.

Bum stepped to the mike and shouted the words that have reverberated through the years in Houston. "This year, I said the road to the Super Bowl went through Pittsburgh," he said, as 55,000 voices came to parade rest and blue and white pompons hung limp. "I'll tell you one damn thing: next year, the road to the Super Bowl goes through Houston."

When the screaming subsided, he wiped tears from his eyes and continued. "I said there's no way they can top the reception we had last year, but let me tell you one damn thing: You've topped it. One year ago, we knocked on the door; this year, we beat on the door, next year, we're gonna kick the sumbitch in."

Players echoed the promise. "I cried in the dressing room because I thought it was a lost cause," defensive end Elvin Bethea shouted into the tumult. "I said I was going to retire, but after this I'm not going to retire."

In Pittsburgh, the Oilers had lost a touchdown catch by receiver Mike Renfro on a hotly disputed official's call in the end zone. Speakers from disc jockeys to politicians hammered that theme, whipping the crowd into a frenzy as it awaited the team, which didn't arrive until 10:25 p.m. The buses pulled into an arena bulging with fans and the throb of the the fight song, played at a deafening pitch. Cheers filled the air for every speaker, including Bud Adams.

"I can't begin to express my appreciation for your support," the owner gurgled. "You're the greatest fans in the world."

Less than a year later, the 11-5 Oilers lost a wild-card playoff to the Raiders in Oakland, and Adams rewarded the fans by firing Phillips, saying he wanted a coach who could take the team to a higher level. Bum never made good on his promise to kick the sumbitch in, but no one blamed him.

The Lone Ranger, Dirty Harry, Superman — they all had a knack for dropping in at the right place at the right time, but none more so than Bum Phillips. If his timing and stage presence had been any better, he would have been Sir Laurence Olivier in boots and a Stetson, with a chaw of Tinsley's Natural Leaf in his cheek, of course. He was a Texan, born 90 miles from Houston in Orange, who had spent almost his entire life in the state, once turning down a chance to follow Paul "Bear" Bryant from Texas A&M to Alabama. Bum took a high school coaching job in Amarillo instead.

He was a real cowboy in the age of the Urban Cowboy, the rawhide ideal of every stock broker and car dealer who could climb into a pair of $600 boots. He was a winner in, of, and for a city of winners when boomtown Houston paved the streets with black gold. If you didn't like Bum, you didn't like Houston or Texas or football and you might be best advised, son, to keep your thoughts to yourself.

He grew up in the malodorous corner of the state the Chamber of Commerce boys like to call the Golden Triangle, attended high school in Beaumont, where his father ran an auto-repair business and kept dairy cows on the side. After he gained his fame, Bum spoke of his father fondly, but he fell out of the mold of his two grandfathers. One of them was ranch boss for a millionaire, and Bum worked cattle for him and scalded and butchered hogs. The other, his paternal grandfather, rode the Chisholm trail at age 13 and worked as a ranch hand for the legendary West Texas cattle king Captain Charles Goodnight.

The young Bum — a sister, two years older, who couldn't pronounce "brother" stuck him with the nickname, one their mother would not use — never thought of his family tree as a pedigree. He loved horses and could have immersed himself in ranch life without a second thought, but he grew up rooted in the same notion that gripped most of his contemporaries. He would finish high school and go to work in one of the area's refineries.

That's exactly the course on which he proceeded, but Bum Phillips wasn't like the other boys, and two seminal events bumped him off that heading before he even got a good layer of grease under his fingernails. One was a three-year hitch fighting the Japanese in the South Pacific that taught him he didn't care for Marine Corps-style discipline.

"I never have liked anything where a guy tried to make me do something," he said. "I don't mind somebody asking me to do something, but the Marines prided themselves on the fact that, 'By God, you're gonna do it because we told you to.' I just don't like for somebody to be bitchin' at me all the time."

After the war, the 21-year-old veteran went home, and he did indeed find a job in a refinery, where he figured to work until retirement. When a supervisor approached him about a contribution to charity, retirement came in a hurry. "I told him I didn't give to that particular charity." Bum suggested giving to another cause, but the company's goal involved 100 percent employee participation in donations to a specific organization, and so was he informed.

"Then tell the man at the gate to have my check ready. I'm leaving." The supervisor suggested he work through Friday to finish the week. "Wednesday's good enough for me," Phillips said. "Just have my check ready."

Heading home in his pickup, he considered his plight. He was newly wed, without job skills, and, now, unemployed. En route, he drove past Lamar College, saw a football practice in progress, and stopped to watch. The coach walked over and asked if he wanted a tryout. Phillips declined, but he later returned, worked out, and accepted a scholarship.

"I wasn't really that interested, but I realized I could go to school on the GI Bill. And this would be something to do until I got a good job." His stint at the two-year school led to a place on the team at Stephen F. Austin University in Nacogdoches, where he played the line, offense and defense, and then to a career in coaching.

For most of it, he should have ridden a camel and lived in a tent. When he joined the Oilers as an assistant coach under Sid Gillman, he accepted his 16th position in less than 30 years. Some of those jobs he left for better ones, some simply because he didn't believe he could make a difference. He gave up the head job at Texas Western (later the University of Texas at El Paso) after one year because he didn't feel he'd ever to be able to recruit successfully there. At that time, as when he declined Bryant's offer to work for him at Alabama, he stepped back down into the high school ranks.

Prestige was never an issue, nor was a career ladder conceived by someone else. Bum loved football and he loved working with young men. He didn't bitch at them and he didn't hang around any place where someone would bitch at him.

Gillman hired him as an assistant with the San Diego Chargers — the first time Phillips had lived outside Texas, other than his time in the Marines — and Bum jumped at the chance to go home when Gillman signed on as coach and general manager of the Oilers. When Gillman gave up one of those titles, he recommended his defensive coordinator. Bud Adams agreed. In the four years prior to Gillman's one full season as head coach, the Oilers had compiled a record of 9-45-2. In that one season, 1974, the team went 7-7. Gillman had the organization moving in the right direction, and Phillips was his hand-picked successor.

It couldn't have hurt that Bum, never one to quibble over dollars, took the job for $125,000 a year. His friend and advisor in financial matters, Houston oilman John Mecom, who would later hire him as coach of the New Orleans Saints at $600,000 a year, said Adams paid Phillips less than some NFL assistant coaches earned. Bum took the top job in January, 1975. Less than three weeks later, Gillman quit as GM, saying he couldn't tolerate Adams's meddling, and Phillips added the general manager's title as well.

At $125,000 for both jobs, Adams had the steal of the league. He also had the coach who would take his team places it had never been and would never see again, at least not while it played in Houston.

Prior to Bum, the Oilers had compiled a record of 86-123-6, but the raw numbers cast the franchise in a much too benevolent light. Since the AFL-NFL merger, the team had put up these records: 3-10-1, 4-9-1, 1-13, 1-13, 7-7. The coach preceding Gillman, Bill Peterson, had come to the Oilers from Rice University, where he had earned his spurs as a pro coach by throwing a chair through a window to motivate his players. Gillman took over a sad-sack organization that had fired the right people and hired the wrong ones at a dizzying pace, becoming the eighth head coach in 14 seasons, ninth if you count Wally Lemm (1961 and 1966-70) twice.

When Bum replaced him, Gillman had put the team on solid footing, but then the Oilers had never steered clear of the next bog of quicksand for very long. They had lost an established and respected pro coach, trading him in for an NFL novice who had never even held a head job at a big-time college. Phillips had spent some time at the University of Houston under Bill Yeoman as well as at Texas A&M, but assistants didn't draw much notice from press and public, even those who could encapsulate the mysteries of life in a pithy sentence or two between toxic streams of tobacco discharge.

Few expected anything but more of the same from the Oilers under Bum. Willie Alexander, a fine defensive back, joined the majority: "When Bum got the job, we all figured, 'What the hell is going on?' He had no head-coaching experience and no one really saw him as head-coaching material. We thought the joke was on us, but without a doubt he was the greatest coach we could have had."

Later, Houston learned the truth of one of the many Bumisms: "I always thought I could coach. I just thought people were poor judges of good coaches."

5

Luv Ya Blue!

In Bum Phillips' six years, the Oilers won 55 games and lost 35 in regular-season play. A team that hadn't made the playoffs since 1969, before the merger, advanced in each of his last three seasons and twice played for the AFC title. Bum's Oilers succeeded in a way that will never be measured by percentages or trophies, however; they symbolized a city rather than merely representing it. On the same weekend Houston lost in Pittsburgh in the conference championship game for the second time, the Rams returned to Los Angeles from Tampa with the NFC title. A crowd of 4,000 greeted them.

Houston embraced its also-rans in a bear hug most champions have never felt from their cities, and Bum and his boys hugged back. Elsewhere, the sports landscape had begun to change as higher pay made athletes more vulnerable and more detached, but the Oilers bellied up to the bar with Joe Six-Pack and drank him under it.

"They certainly were a relaxed bunch," the coach said of his men. "They weren't quiet. You know, Dan [Pastorini] wasn't the kind of guy you'd lend your new sports car to. They was always able to have fun. But, heck, money was flowin' free and everybody was successful and there was the team and the Urban Cowboy and Gilley's. Everything kind of came together at one time."

The Oilers and the town coalesced, to use a fancier word, in the era that came to be known as "Luv Ya Blue!" Earl Campbell was no Herodotus, but mangled syntax wasn't about to keep a man who mangled linebackers out of commercials. In a couple, he just grinned. In another, he had one line: "Skoal, brother." If he wasn't as quick on the draw as his coach, Campbell was every bit as much a Texan. His mufti was boots and jeans and an easy grin and, like Bum, he never doubted where he fit.

When he signed his first contract, Adams handed him the keys to a new Lincoln Continental. The next day, he returned the car. "Mr. Adams," he said, "Mama thinks it would look awful bad to drive that big Lincoln back to Tyler, so I guess I'll stay in my old pickup. Here's the keys."

Pastorini, who came from California, ruled over the bar scene like a Mardi Gras king. Bum's players always had plenty in reserve for extracurricular activities. They practiced crisply, but never for long. He figured gaps between drills would lead to visitin' on the field, and as much as he liked visitin' he considered it an after-hours pursuit.

Bum was ever accessible to the media, but every reporter knew to catch him before five, after which time he was gone to his horses. In an age of buttoned-down coaches who wore bags under their eyes in the way an old soldier parades his Purple Heart, another rookie head coach might have squeezed himself into the mold of a Landry or Noll or Shula, but Bum was Bum. He did make one concession to decorum. Not once did he wear his Stetson in the Astrodome. His mama had always told him to remove his hat in the house.

Apparently, she never instructed him not to spit on the carpet, but then previous Houston teams had left far darker stains on the Astroturf than he ever could.

Bum got on famously with the press, even though his most dazzling display of a comic genius's sense of timing came at the expense of a reporter. Dale Robertson of the *Houston Post* had incurred the wrath of Pastorini, who refused to speak to him. When Robertson circumvented the embargo by listening to taped interviews conducted by friends in radio and quoting from those, the quarterback became infuriated.

Phillips was speaking with a Pittsburgh newspaperman outside the locker one day when the fellow observed that the Oilers didn't have the grinding friction between team and media of many other NFL clubs. "Naw," said Bum, "we don't have no problems like that." At that instant, Robertson came flying through the door, propelled by a Pastorini fist, and landed at their feet. "Til now," Bum added.

The crew-cut icon made his share of commercials, too, many at no charge for old friends from whom he had bought boots or hats for years. As in the matter of giving to charities on the job, however, he never relaxed his standards. He drank beer, not so publicly as his players but, on plane rides home, with unsurpassed thirst and determination. But pounding suds was one thing, endorsing them another. He once turned down $15,000 to do a beer commercial.

"I keep thinking some kid of 16 who looked up to me might hear me endorsing some beer and have one too many one night and crack up his car," he said. "That's why I could never do it."

Neither did his principles bend in favor of the owner. Adams, who traveled on his own jet when he attended road games, routinely sent business associates and other guests on the team's chartered 727. They joined Phillips and his coaches in the first-class cabin — until Bud's largesse squeezed Bum's players. Adams packed off 22 cronies on one flight, and when they spilled over into coach, they deprived several athletes of an open middle seat. Declaring, "I'm more interested in the comfort of my players than I am my comfort and the comfort of a bunch of freeloaders," Phillips changed the seating arrangement so that all 22 starters and two special-teamers filled first class and coaches and cronies took up the rear along with medical, equipment, and film personnel, front-office employes, and the media.

"They're all big men," he said of the players. "You can't expect three 270-pound men to squeeze in side-by-side either goin' to a game or comin' back when they're all banged up. The seats are too small. Think what kind of attitude this team would have if we squeezed them all into coach seats, then expected them to play football when we got where we were going."

Adams acquiesced, but he and his coach never enjoyed a warm relationship. One might have assumed otherwise since, beyond their families, both men's passions appeared to be football and ranching. In the end, their differences were more profound.

Bum liked to dig in up to his elbows whether working players or horses, mending a fence or birthing a calf. Bud observed his holdings from a distance, never investing more of his money or himself than he thought would fetch a return. Perhaps his true passion was collecting. He crammed his mammoth office with Indian artifacts, Western art, a Japanese garden. And he collected businesses.

Whatever chill cut the humidity, it didn't affect the play of the team. Adams was essentially a disengaged owner and Phillips, a career assistant, slipped into the role of head coach and GM as easily as changing his shirt. He wanted control. "I'd make a good one-term politician," he drawled. "I'm afraid I wouldn't get re-elected, 'cause there ain't but one way to do something and it's got nothin' to do with gettin' votes."

His way worked for his players, who would have followed Bum into a blast furnace, and did several times, in Pittsburgh. In each of his last four seasons, the Oilers actually split their two regular-season games with the Steelers. The playoffs were a different matter, but the wonder was that Bum's boys twice made it to the conference championship round. Those Pittsburgh teams featured Terry Bradshaw, Franco Harris, Lynn Swann, John Stallworth, Mean Joe Greene, Jack Ham, and Jack Lambert. Houston sent Earl Campbell plunging into the rest of the future Hall of Fame.

As the Tyler Rose was sweeping league MVP honors for three years beginning in 1978, the Oilers did deploy other Pro Bowl-caliber talent. Robert Brazile, Curley Culp, and Elvin Bethea were fixtures on defense and Leon Gray, Kenny Burrough, and Billy "White Shoes" Johnson all had their moment in the sun when postseason honors were passed out, as did kicker Toni Fritsch. Compared to the Pittsburgh colossus, however, they were a scruffy lot.

On the team that came closest to making the Super Bowl, in 1979, 22 players arrived either as undrafted free agents or off the waiver wire. Kick returner Johnny Dirden had been driving a cement truck (and Carl Roaches, another return man who arrived the next season, an ice cream truck). Defensive end Jimmy Young had been a fireman, and Guido Merkens, who played receiver and defensive back, had been hanging out and playing city-league softball.

"We had a lot of people," said Bum, "who came down knowin' that if they could make it anywhere in the NFL, they could make it here. We didn't care about how big they were or if they went to Notre Dame or USC. We just wanted football players."

If they could play, they could stay. Phillips plucked Steve Baumgartner off waivers in 1977 and moved him from defensive end to linebacker. "I made my living on special teams," he said, "but on that team, everyone got the feeling that what they were doing was a major part of the game. No matter what you did, everybody was respected for what they could do for the team."

The magic-carpet ride began in 1978. In April, Phillips traded tight end Jimmie Giles and three draft choices to Tampa Bay for the No. 1 pick in the draft and selected Campbell, the Heisman Trophy winner from the University of Texas. In his first game, a loss to Atlanta, he ran for 137 yards and gained another 73 after catching a short pass. In the fifth game of the season, in Cleveland, the Oilers fell behind, 10-0, then fought back to win, 16-13, on a late bomb from Pastorini to Kenny Burrough.

Rich Caster, who caught a 41-yard scoring pass in the rally, felt something special had happened. "That Cleveland game made us realize we could win in any situation," he said. "It felt like a significant game, which we hadn't played a lot of to that point."

From then on, they were all big. The networks had discovered Bum, and the woebegone Oilers were now Monday Night Football stars. They beat the Steelers in Pittsburgh, 24-17, for their first prime-time victory ever — not that they had been in demand to that time, with four appearances in eight years — beat the Patriots on the road, 26-23, after trailing, 23-0, and went home for a Monday night game with Miami.

Campbell was known for sticking his helmet into a linebacker's chest on a burst up the middle and churning his piston thighs for more yards until three men bulldogged him to earth. This was a force of nature unleashed in foul temper, and even the Good Lord must have marveled at what He had wrought. Game after game, opposing defenders swore no back could deal and absorb punishment on that scale and last long in the league.

Earl brought with him from college a habit of remaining down after a play, at first causing fans to fear each time that he was broken beyond repair. When it was pointed out to his coach that his prized recruit got up slowly, Bum said, "Yeah, but he goes down slow, too." Campbell was merely taking a hard-earned blow after his violent collisions.

The Dolphins had reluctantly participated in too many of those by the fourth quarter and were bracing for more when Earl said, "Skoal, brother," sprinted right, turned the corner, and outran the world for 81 yards and a 35-31 victory. Bum's boys had by-durn arrived, right there on national tee-vee.

A 10-6 season produced a wild card, and the Oilers darkened the door of the playoffs for the first time since 1969. They went on the road to beat the Dolphins and overwhelm the Patriots. Before the upset in Miami, Pastorini had fluid drained from a knee and an elbow and strapped on a flak jacket to protect tender ribs. Of all the Oilers, he had the greatest investment after nine years of losses outnumbered only by sledgehammer shots to the head.

"That was a game you have to work nine years for," he said. "I thought Bum was thinking about not playing me, but after suffering through those 1-13 years, I had to play."

The 34-5 loss to the Steelers the following week did nothing to prick Boomtown's balloon. Campbell gained 1,450 yards and ran the table of postseason honors: All-Rookie Team, Rookie of the Year, Pro Bowl, All-Pro, AFC Player of the Year, NFL Offensive Player of the

Year, and league MVP. In Houston, it was considered a glaring over-sight that he had not been named king.

Another significant event occurred in 1978, although it went almost without notice at the time. Bud Adams named Ladd Herzeg senior vice president and chief administrative officer of the franchise.

The next year, Campbell ran for 1,697 yards and the team won 11 games. Because Pittsburgh won 12, the Oilers were a wild card again. They beat Denver at home and won in San Diego with Gifford Nielsen and Rob Carpenter filling in for Pastorini and Campbell.

Rich Ellender joined the team to return kicks that season and never called for a fair catch: "When I got to Houston, I asked Bum what he expected from me. He said, 'I don't want you to fumble, and every yard you move the ball toward the goal line, that's one less yard Earl will have to get by himself.' So I wasn't thinking average. I was thinking, to heck with that, let's do it for the team." It was Team Schmaltz, and proud of it.

Carpenter, who would move on to the New York Giants, said, "I was around some success after I left Houston but my experience with the Oilers still is the most enjoyable. Nobody cared about whose name got in the paper or this guy's making more money or that guy's got the best-looking girlfriend. We just cared about each other and that was an extension of Bum. I just knew that when Bum was fired that team would fall apart. There's certain people in life you just can't replace."

The second loss in a title game in Pittsburgh went down much harder. Late in the third quarter, with the Steelers up by seven, Pastorini arched a pass for Mike Renfro in the right corner of the end zone and the receiver tucked the ball in as he touched his toes down just inside the sideline. Field judge Donald Orr hesitated, then gave a weak signal for incompletion.

"When I stood up," said Renfro, "I knew it was close, but I knew I had caught the ball and I was already celebrating. Then I turned and saw the two biggest eyeballs I've ever seen in my life. He knew he wasn't ready to make the call. He blew it."

Commissioner Pete Rozelle later admitted Orr missed the call. Fortunately for the league, the Steelers held Campbell to 15 yards on 17 slips over a frozen field and won by 14. In Houston, the what-ifs persisted, but the Steelers had satisfied the rest of the country. Maybe Bum, too.

"Playing Pittsburgh," he said, "is like eating ice cream on a hot summer day. Sometime before you can get it all in your mouth, it gets all over you."

The second blowout in the Astrodome upon the team's return set a record for a municipal hug and kiss that might stand unto eternity. It's a fair guess, anyway, that Bud Adams will never see anything to match it.

Even though Bum had been through a warm-up a year earlier and had an idea of what to expect, he wasn't prepared for his reaction to the crowd, and out spilled the line about kicking the sumbitch in.

"When people have been sittin' there in the stands for six hours waitin' on you," he said, "and you just got beat, you don't tell 'em that next year you're gonna try harder. I hadn't really thought about what I was gonna say. It just came out. And I really felt we could kick it in. I really felt like we could go through Pittsburgh."

But while the city would have excused him the Luv-Ya-Bluest of language, Bum had disappointed himself. "I have no excuse for usin' that kind of language," he said three weeks later. "There is no excuse. I apologize. If that situation came up again, I'd bite my tongue first. If my daddy was alive and heard me say that, he'd have whupped me alongside the head." Under the Code of Bum: "You take off your hat in an elevator, in the house, and in the presence of ladies. And you don't use bad language around ladies. Those are old customs and I'm not ashamed of them."

In 1980, Campbell ran for 1,934 yards, and the Oilers again won 11 games. This time, Cleveland won 11 and the tie-breaker for the division title, relegating Houston to wild-card status again. The highlight was a December skunking of the Steelers in the Astrodome, 6-0, that knocked them out of the playoffs. The lowlight was the 27-7 pounding by Oakland in the wild-card round. And then, of course, the firing of Bum.

The coach had already taken a beating for declaring he would never trade Pastorini — "Dan's like a son to me" — and then shipping him to Oakland for Kenny Stabler. Some time later, Bum revealed that Pastorini had come to him after he was booed as he was carried off his home field on a stretcher and reminded him of a promise. Bum had always told his players he would never hold them against their will. The quarterback demanded a trade, the coach told him to cool off for a while. Pastorini returned three days later and pressed the issue, and Bum relented.

Stabler threw for 13 touchdowns with 28 interceptions, and Campbell watched his candle blown out. He would have but one more season of greatness. Those who had predicted a short career for a man who carried more than 20 times a game and took multiple hits on every haul were proved right.

There would be no party in the Astrodome this time, and Bum was under fire for a predictable offense. Still, sacking the coach of an 11-5 team that had in the two previous seasons fallen a game short of the Super Bowl was unthinkable — until three days after the Oakland loss, New Year's Eve.

6

CRASH LANDING

Bum probably took his firing better than anyone else — at first. Perhaps his most-quoted Bumism was, "There's two kinds of coaches, them that's been fired and them that's gonna be fired." He meant it, and lived it. He never dwelt in fear of losing a job or in dread of returning to coaching in high school if that number came up. He was shocked, he admitted, and he cried when he told his son and assistant coach, Wade, the news over the phone.

"What hurt the most," he said, "was having to leave a team I thought was potentially a great team. I had to leave a group of guys I really, really loved. I had a close feeling for those guys because of all the great times we had together." He was not bitter. When he took the job, he had said, "I don't have much more than a handshake and that's O.K. with me." When he lost it, he thanked Adams for seven years and told him, "We're even." In public comments, he said repeatedly that the owner was entirely within his rights to make a change.

While hardly unemotional, his parting from the Oilers was as simple as that. It was the aftermath that got messy. Ladd Herzeg timed the announcement brilliantly. A city riding a "kick the door in" high had come down with a crash with the loss in Oakland. Still, the reaction to the sacking of the most successful coach in the team's history and a folk hero, to boot, burned with the fire of Shakespearean passion and less elegant prose.

Herzeg, who was never unprepared in those sober days, countered with a flurry of charts and graphs straight out of the devil's own audit. The CPA demonstrated that Bum's Oilers were too old, had undermined the future by trading away high draft choices, lacked discipline, and suffered offensive stagnation because Phillips refused to hire a coordinator. None of his charts indicated the team had gone 11-5.

In Bum's view, firing a coach was fair; smearing his name was not, especially when he was interested in another NFL job. He was particularly disturbed by the charge that his team lacked discipline, as evidenced by the 80 alleged rules violations, only two of which were punished by fines. That indictment and the refusal to name an offensive coordinator underpinned the conviction of Bum Phillips.

"It's an obvious attempt to discredit me," Bum said. "They want to kill me, not just fire me. If this keeps up, he [Adams] will cost me the New Orleans job. Then, if I don't get it, he can sit back and say, 'See, I told you he was a no-good coach.'

"He [Adams] said something about the players havin' 80 infractions and I only fined them for two. I don't know how many fines there were. Maybe that many, maybe three or four or six. But I ain't changed from the other years when we were 10-4 or 5-9 or playing Pittsburgh for the championship. In a city this big, if a player calls in and tells me he has car trouble or his wife is sick, I don't mind if he's late. I'll never change on that. All I ask is that they call in.

"Why's he even bringing this up? When he fired me, I only said dignified things. I said it was right for him to fire me. Why can't he be dignified? Why does he have to get into all of these things? I'll tell you why: because they say nobody ever becomes a head coach after he leaves the Oilers. With him, I can understand why. There's no tellin' what he's told Mr. Mecom about me."

The lack-of-discipline charge bothered him the most. "The thing I want to know is, how the hell did he know about it? He never went to a meeting, never went to a practice, never went to a road game last season. If things were so bad, why didn't he call me in September and tell me about it then? Why does he try to insult me now? I think he must have hired a spy to report things like that. He'd do somethin' like that. When he was havin' problems with a reporter a few years ago, he thought about puttin' a private detective on the reporter. I think I was the one who talked him out of that.

"I just don't understand why he's doin' this to me. I never talked about some of the things he does. I wasn't the one who complained two years ago when he offered us a ham or a turkey after the season when other coaching staffs got big (cash) bonuses. I didn't even say anything this year when he cut out the ham or turkey for the coaches and gave them to everybody else out here.

"Believe me, if he wants to keep this up, I can get into a lot of things. He complained to me about this year's highlights film being too big a promotion for me. I agreed with him. I've told the NFL Films people that, too. But I also told him, 'Mr. Adams, NFL Films shoots the film and markets it the best way they know how. I don't have anything to do with that.'"

Many surmised that Adams's jealousy over the Phillips cult of personality triggered the firing. In fact, Herzeg had cultivated that seed in his effort to wrest control of the team. When Bum had negotiated a three-year contract early in 1978, he was already locked in a power struggle with Herzeg, who was campaigning for authority over trades and the draft. In that instance, Bum won, but he traded off a five-year package for a three-year contract that gave him the final say on all personnel matters. Herzeg said tersely, "The ballclub felt that a three-year contract at this time was all we were willing to offer."

One of Bum's motivations to win a Super Bowl, or to reach one at the least, was that it would strengthen his position. The loss to the Raiders as that three-year contract expired presented Herzeg with the opening he needed, and he blew through the hole like Campbell bursting up the middle. It wouldn't have proved a shock if he had hung a whistle around his neck and taken over the team on the field. Given his low regard for coaches, however, he probably considered the position beneath him.

Herzeg believed he could put the Oilers in the Super Bowl with Machiavellian maneuvering in football's flesh bazaars, and that the coach was almost incidental. Once, when his name came up, New York Giants GM George Young said, "Some people are looking for a fair trade that helps both teams. Others are always out to screw somebody."

If Pastorini hadn't succumbed to hurt feelings after standing up under all the punishment to his body and demanded a trade, if the Oilers had won the tie-breaker and avoided Oakland in the wild-card round, if Adams had received better potty-training, the course of history might have been different. Houston might even still have a pro football team.

Bum moved on to New Orleans. Herzeg took charge of the Oilers. Adams said, "Our discipline problems were eating at my craw pretty good. Bum was really the only one who could stop it. I'll say one thing: Ed Biles won't put up with it. That doesn't necessarily mean we're going to win this season, but we will have discipline."

Biles's goose-stepping Oilers went 7-9 in 1981. Thereafter, the team didn't win more than five games in a season until 1987. With the Saints, Bum acquired several of his former Houston players, including an over-the-hill Campbell, for whom he gave up a No. 1 draft choice. If loyalty endures, however, magic loses its fizz and turns into stale beer.

At a luncheon shortly after he took the job, a priest prayed, "Oh, Lord, when Israel was in trouble, you sent them three wise men from the East. I hope you know what you're doing now, dear Lord, sending us one Bum from the West."

Injuries and drug problems plagued Bum's New Orleans teams, which never made the playoffs in his five years or finished better than 8-8. Financial difficulties forced Mecom to sell the franchise to Tom Benson, and a beer bath convinced Bum it was time to mosey. He had planned to leave with Mecom, but the sale didn't close until two months before training camp, too short a time for Benson to put a coaching staff together, so Bum stayed on for one final season.

"Injuries had us down again," he said, "and we lost a game to Seattle that we shouldn't've lost. When I was walkin' off the field, in an alley between the stands, the same fat lady who had thrown beer on me the game before threw beer on me again. I just said to myself, 'I ain't walkin' in this place again.' I guess if that had happened 10 years earlier, I would have just gotten mad and come back and done better, but that hurt my feelings. I was just tired of it. It was time to do somethin' else."

He walked away with three years and a guaranteed $1.35 million left on his contract. "I told Tom Benson he wasn't going to get a better coach but it was time for him to get a different coach. It was to the point he was goin' to have to defend me to the press and fans or let me down, and he wasn't goin' to let me down. He needed those people, but he was goin' to alienate them if he defended me. When I told him I was leavin,' I told him he didn't owe me a penny. I don't think Tom would've fired me, ever, but even if he had, I wouldn't've let him pay me.

"Way I see it, a man don't earn it, it don't belong to him. Sure, I could've used the million dollars, but I wasn't desperate. This is a league that has a great retirement plan for coaches. When you coach as long as I did, and if you make as much as I did in your last five years, you earn the maximum, and the maximum ain't bad. Under their retirement plan, they'll be payin' me $90,000 a year for the rest of my life. Man can't make it on $90,000, his livin' expenses are too high."

Ten years after Adams fired him, Bum returned to the Oilers as a color commentator on radio broadcasts. Herzeg, of course, was gone by then. Just as Herzeg had prevailed on Bud to fire him, Mike McClure, the marketing man, convinced the owner to bring him back. As with the down-home musings of other countrified philosophers, Bum's didn't fit in a broadcast.

Even working with his former player and good friend, Gifford Nielsen, the timing was always a little off, and Bum wasn't good at making his mouth move when he figured there was nothing that needed saying. Still, McClure's move proved a good one because fans adored Bum as much as ever and ached for a warm "Luv Ya Blue!" fuzzy.

When he came back, he minced no words as to why he was fired: "Ladd Herzeg."

"He wanted to run the doggone team. He wanted to make the decisions on who to draft, trade, and waive. He wanted to run the team and decide who to play, really. All Bud did was what the people he hired influenced him to do. It's a guy's right to run his business like he thinks is best. If he thinks he can get somebody better than me, it's his right as an owner.

"I didn't want Ladd Herzeg telling me how to run my team. I wanted the right to make that decision. I don't think for a second that Bud really cared if I had an offensive coordinator. I think somebody convinced him, meaning Ladd."

And that old wound still hadn't closed. "I didn't like the fact that he had to try to dig up numbers to prove I wasn't a good football coach. It was their right to fire me, but don't try to kill me, too. Let me be gone. You don't have to try to discredit me. I thought that was really bad. I just didn't think it was fair, and he [Herzeg] was the author of it."

As for the offensive coordinator issue, nine of the 10 previous Super Bowl champions had not employed one, and 18 of the league's 28 teams had none in that 1980 season. Among those were four of the six division winners. That year, the Oilers had scrimmaged with a new quarterback, lost four starters to injury, and won 11 games, tying for the team's first division title since the merger. On the discipline front, the Oilers had no more and no less than in any other season. They had raised hell in the bars and in the team hotel on the night before games, and they had raised hell on the field.

Bud took something precious away from Bum when he fired him, but he gave away something valuable of his own. Under Phillips, the formerly faceless Oilers had an identity. Across the country, fans delighted in the slow-talkin' wrangler of a coach who wouldn't take his team to Cleveland early in the week to become acclimated for a play-off game because "You cain't practice bein' miserable." Bum made several appearances in Pittsburgh each off-season, and could have done more if he'd had the time and inclination. Winning hearts and souls elsewhere was puny stuff, however, compared to claiming them in Texas.

For the only period in the existence of the franchise, the Oilers hit America's Team with a forearm shiver. Of the 69 stations on the team's radio network in 1980 — it was the second most extensive in the NFL — 67 had signed on since Bum became coach. Newspapers in Austin, San Antonio, and elsewhere that had virtually ignored the Oilers while staffing Cowboys games began sending reporters to Houston. Before and after, Bud Adams's team was treated as a poor relation of the Cowboys even in the town where it trained.

"This was 99 percent Cowboys country before the Oilers started training here in 1978," said a newspaperman in San Angelo, west of Dallas. "It got to be 50-50 the first year. After that, this was Oilers country, mostly because of Bum. The people loved him."

A Houston woman returned from a trip to her native Lubbock in West Texas and reported, "Only the Cowboys used to get regular newspaper and television coverage. Groups arranged bus trips to Dallas for games. No one was interested in going to Houston to see the Oilers. No one even seemed to care if Oilers games were televised in Lubbock.

"It changed after Bum was hired. The Oilers started getting coverage equal to what the Cowboys received. People talked as much about the Oilers as the Cowboys the last year or two. Then Bum came to Lubbock to make a speech. When they tried to give him a $1,500 honorarium, he suggested there was probably a Lubbock charity that could put the money to better use than he could. Everybody in town was talking about what he did. By then, he was bigger than the Cowboys. If he'd stayed in Lubbock, he could've been elected mayor."

"Sometimes," said Pastorini, "I look back at those times and I think I should have just walked away from the game after 1979. It was the top, the best of the best, and it couldn't get any better. You had people from every walk of life and all over the country and we all really had a mutual admiration for each other. There was just some intangible bonding that we had that just seemed to work. We played hurt and pulled for each other. The highlight of my whole career, period, bar none, was playing on those teams. That made it all worthwhile, even though we didn't quite get through the door."

The NFL rarely misses a chance to schedule a grudge match. The season after he was fired, Bum returned to the Astrodome with the Saints. His team won the game and a capacity crowd raised the roof with an outpouring of affection for the ol' cowpoke, who remembered the day for an incident that explained why Carl Mauck stayed around past his prime.

"We were together as a team," Bum said. "You fight that guy, you fight me, too. We had togetherness. There was just a feeling among those players. We had (22) free agents. A lot of them were good football players that didn't find it out until they came to us.

"You take a guy like Carl Mauck. I've been friends with Mauck ever since he played for San Diego. We've always hit it off just perfect, and he's really a close friend of mine. I'll give you an example of how competitive he was. In 1981, we came back over here to play the Oilers. I was on the Saints sideline. The Oilers ran a screen pass and Mauck pulled on the play. He ended up pretty close to our sideline when he hit the ground. I looked at Mauck and said, 'How in the hell did you get way out here?' He rolled over and Wade was standin' right there. Mauck jumped up and cussed out Wade. Wade said, 'I didn't say that. The old man said that.' Then Mauck cussed me out.

"I mean, he was mad. That friendship went out the window. It was a football game and he didn't give a damn if it was his daddy or God standing there. If you were on that sideline, you were against him."

7

THE ROUND-
BELLIED
RASPUTIN

Hard by Interstate 35 in San Marcos, the American Utilitarian motel featured a laundry room but lacked that *je ne sais quoi* Pauline Holovak was seeking. The roar of 18-wheelers hauling down the four-lane from Austin to San Antonio competed with the shrieks of children at the swimming pool, excited after their visit to Ralph the Swimming Pig at Aquarena Springs.

The wife of Oilers general manager Mike Holovak had spent one training camp at the motel and resolved to find more suitable accommodations. She located a bed-and-breakfast on a leafy lane in town and introduced herself to the proprietress, who asked what brought her to Swimming Pig City in the hot shimmer of summer.

"Oh, you're with the Oilers," the woman said. "Do you know Mr. Herzeg? He stayed with us last year. He checked in for a weekend and said Mrs. Herzeg was coming. He wanted me to get him cham-

pagne and caviar, certain brands he specified. When I told him I did-
n't think I could find them in San Marcos, he gave me $100 bills and
told me to drive to Austin and get them there. Then the next week,
he came back and did the same thing, but it was another Mrs. Herzeg.
And the next week . . ."

Ladd K. Herzeg had a big brain, a big wad of hundreds, and a big
backside. He enjoyed putting all three on display.

When he succeeded in collaboration with defensive coordinator
Ed Biles in deposing Bum Phillips as general manager and coach,
Herzeg saw unfolded before him an open field on which to perform
his shiftiest moves. For a man who viewed life as a succession of
intrigues in which he always outwitted the canny-but-flawed operative
on the other side, this was heaven, or as close as he was likely to get.
Already the No. 2 man in each of Bud Adams's companies, Herzeg
knew the way to his employer's shriveled heart was through his
expanding wallet, and Herzeg did perform.

A man of considerable talent in the financial arena, he made a pile
for Bud, and for himself. Perhaps that's why he was able, after he left
Adams in a beef over salary, to travel the world, sending mocking postcards from exotic resorts to the mother of a child he fathered while
married to another woman. He mailed many cards, but never a cent
in child support.

Herzeg embarrassed Houston on many occasions, but never his
boss, who explained after Herzeg got drunk on champagne, slapped
a newspaper columnist and wrecked his expensive BMW, "I know
Ladd pretty well. I know his good points and I know his bad points.
I used to think you couldn't have any so-called reprobates or bad guys
on your football team, but I've changed my mind. You can't have all

good guys, whether it's players, coaches, or staff. Getting the job done is what matters, and Ladd's done a good job."

The beefy accountant who kept his wife around to tie his shoes filled Adams's bill admirably. He made money, and he made some shrewd moves that brought to Houston several talented players, notably quarterback Warren Moon, a hot property pursued by several NFL clubs after he confiscated every passing record worth having in the Canadian Football League. Herzeg's problems — other than those related to bubbles and Bubbles — turned on his selection of coaches.

Perhaps those difficulties shouldn't have been surprising, considering the low esteem in which he held coaches. "Coaching an NFL team should be easy," he said over dinner one night early in his tenure as GM. "All you have to do is look around the league at what the successful coaches are doing and copy it."

The copycats he hired lacked even the modest skills he required, for in Herzeg's eight seasons as GM the Oilers compiled a 42-78 record, including 2-1 by replacement players in the strike season of 1987. Biles (8-23) was followed on an interim basis by Chuck Studley (2-8), who gave way to Hugh Campbell (8-22), replaced by Jerry Glanville (24-25 at the time Herzeg left). Studley merely kept the seat warm in a season Biles began with an 0-6 record. In the case of each of the others, the appointment was the result of one of Herzeg's grand conspiracies.

Biles won his stripes by ratting out his pal Phillips. With the help of politician/linebacker Gregg Bingham, Biles delivered to Herzeg the list of 80 rules violations Adams used as a pretext for firing Bum. Campbell, at the time the coach of the Los Angeles Express of the United States Football League, had won five Grey Cups with the Edmonton Eskimos. More importantly for Herzeg's purposes, he had coached Moon in Canada and had a good relationship with the quarterback, the signing of whom became an obsession with Herzeg.

The general manager swore when he hired Campbell the decision was independent of his pursuit of Moon. He swore when he fired him after less than two seasons he had signed him only as part of his scheme to lure the quarterback to Houston. Herzeg brought to mind the boxing promoter Bob Arum. Confronted with the assertion that his version of events was opposite of the one he had given the day before, Arum said, "O.K. So yesterday I lied. Today I'm telling the truth."

Herzeg's playing career ended in high school in his native Ohio. He claimed to have attended the University of Hawaii on a football scholarship, only to have his career snuffed by a serious knee injury. The school has no record of his ever playing there. The only limitation he admitted was an inability to evaluate talent. That he conceded tacitly by hiring Mike Holovak as personnel chief.

A former pro player and coach, Holovak had acquired a reputation as a wizard in the draft, one he lived up to with the Oilers. A workaholic who cared little for money and an intensely loyal man, Holovak brought with him a network of connections around the league and as keen an eye for football ability as ever squinted across a field. Herzeg hired Holovak six weeks after Phillips was deposed, and despite drafts depleted of picks in the high rounds by Phillips trades in the first two years, Holovak found football players. Herzeg never located anyone to coach them.

By the time Herzeg fired him, Biles was simpering. In the strike year of 1982, the Oilers went 1-8. In '83, Adams made his first training-camp appearance in three years and gave Biles a limited vote of confidence. "If we can break even this year," he said, "I'll feel we've been very successful." The owner also vowed to remain in the background: "I haven't had any involvement in the last 10 years. I don't intend to get involved. I don't know what I could offer except maybe filling up that big old jacuzzi."

The team lost its first six games the next season, the last of those against Denver in the Astrodome. I had been critical of Biles in my column in the *Houston Chronicle*, and he knew another broadside was coming. After his postgame press conference in the locker room, he took me aside. I expected an explosion; instead, I heard a whimper. The Oilers had enjoyed a rare chance at victory late in the game when quarterback Gifford Nielsen threw an interception.

"Can you believe the pass that guy threw on the sideline?" Biles whined. "We had that game won. Can you believe that pass?"

That proved to be Biles's final game. After Studley served out the rest of that season's sentence, the Campbell era quickly took on the look of Hitler's Russian front. The new coach soon became convinced Herzeg was undermining him by expressing his misgivings in public and talking to players behind his back. On both counts, he was right.

After Campbell's first game, Herzeg complained to the press about a roster switch in which the coach brought back a reserve running back he had cut a week earlier. "That doesn't make any sense at all to me," Herzeg said. "I'm perplexed about the situation. I think it shows indecisiveness on the coaches' part, just like our game plan on Sunday."

Whatever the wisdom of airing his grievances, Herzeg was right about one thing: Campbell was out of his league. Like Biles before him, he would never hold another NFL job. Some years later, on a radio talk show I hosted, Pro Bowl defensive lineman Ray Childress responded to a question on what practices were like when Campbell ran the team: "Mostly, we stood around for a couple of hours, then we went home."

After a rare victory late in the 1985 season, which the team had opened with five losses in six games, Campbell began his day-after press conference by saying, "I cannot tolerate intervention of the type that leads to confusion. It also leads to poor morale and the demise of the program. I feel quite strongly something can and will be done, but we can't do it without every arm of the organization respecting the responsibility and integrity of one another." Two games later, he was history.

Campbell, a decent if overmatched sort, had tried repeatedly to get an audience with the owner to discuss his problems with the GM. Adams never returned his calls.

Campbell left town after his sacking in December saying he didn't know Adams well enough to pass any judgment on him. He'd seen the big boss only once since May.

At the public lynching, Herzeg said, "I'm ready to acknowledge that hiring Hugh Campbell was the worst mistake of my professional career." As to specific reasons for the firing, he said, "I'm not going to get into that. I have a great deal of sensitivity toward Hugh Campbell's family. He has a wife and children who are all affected by this."

And Herzeg was a great believer in family values, as we shall see.

8

MAN IN BLACK

Next case: Palladin in elevator shoes. Jerry Glanville, the nutty professor of football, turned out from chin to toe (only about five feet) every game day in unrelenting black. This he accessorized brilliantly with a silver belt buckle as big as a football. Some wondered if he might show up one day with a couple of washed-up defensive tackles pushing it around in front of him in a wheelbarrow.

What critics in Paris or Milan might say of this ensemble we'll never know, but in Philadelphia one fan registered his vote as Glanville was walking off the Veterans Stadium field by nailing him in the chest with a half-eaten hoagie. Wardrobe aside, of course, he did evoke that kind of reaction.

Herzeg saw in Glanville, as he had in Biles before him, a deceitfulness he prized more than evaporating ink. While both emerged from the job of defensive coordinator, Herzeg didn't need any dirt from Glanville to get rid of Campbell, who didn't enjoy one-tenth of Phillips' popularity. By that time, what's more, Herzeg had Adams so completely spellbound that Bud might not have returned Campbell's calls because he didn't recognize his coach's name. Seldom, if ever, has an owner honored a pledge to remain aloof from the running of his team as faithfully as Bud.

Like Biles, Glanville had cultivated Herzeg, and there was no question the defense had outperformed the offense. With two games left in the 1985 season, the GM pink-slipped Campbell and gave Glanville the job on an interim basis, proclaiming the job was his for keeps if the team won those final two. This was one of the dumbest things Herzeg ever said while sober.

The Oilers stood 5-9 at the time and had lost their last two and four of the previous five games. Four of the five victories had come at home and both remaining games were on the road. Anyone who could levitate that litter of drowned puppies into winners should have been allowed to retire from coaching and proceed directly to the network television booth.

They lost those games by an aggregate score of 62-37, earning Glanville the job anyway. Oh, Herzeg mounted the obligatory "exhaustive search," interviewing just about everyone who could toot a whistle without tripping over the cord. One of the finalists was Paul Hackett, an assistant with the San Francisco 49ers. "I feel if you're going to hire somebody from within the organization," he said, "you should just go ahead and do it and not waste my time."

After scouring the country, Adams was giddy with the man he and Herzeg had discovered standing on the corner. "We wanted someone to kick the players in the butt," he said, dealing one last kick of his own to the laid-back Campbell, "and Jerry's a motivator, the man we believe can take the Oilers to the Super Bowl."

He added, "I don't want y'all to laugh about that."

Us?

Bud said he planned a more active role in running the club, thrilling the masses.

The owner also predicted an immediate trip to the playoffs. The team responded in 1986 by winning its opener and losing the next eight games. After complaining that Campbell never delivered the wide-open offense he promised, Herzeg watched Glanville send backs plowing into the line until their ears rang like cathedral bells.

Moon, the big-ticket passer, handed off and chafed, and finally spoke out. His coach, he complained, ordered him each week to keep the ball on the ground until the team fell two touchdowns behind and then asked him to pull out a victory with a miracle passing attack.

Glanville had turned the Oilers into an extension of his ego, unleashing a pound-it-out offense and a defense Al Capone could have loved; the team passed the dreaded Raiders for the league lead in penalties so fast that Al Davis must have thought a preacher had subverted his kids. The Oilers' special teams violated every taboo in the game, including trying to maim the opponent's placement specialist on kickoffs.

Glanville rewarded the man who fired off the cheapest shots each week with an army helmet, and a few players with the most stir-fried brains actually wore it onto the field for pregame warmups the following week. The coach was having the time of his life playing Mr. Macho and sparring with the press, but at 1-8 Herzeg must have told him his act would play better with a few victories. Glanville turned Moon loose and the team won four of its last seven games, still failing to validate Bud's prediction.

By 1987, Holovak's drafting had assembled so much talent it might have overcome even Campbell's coaching. Moon threw to Drew Hill and Ernest Givins and handed off to Mike Rozier behind a line that included perennial Pro Bowl players Bruce Matthews and Mike Munchak. Childress and linebacker Al Smith anchored a defense good enough to rage through the siege of penalties. By '88, the Oilers sent eight players to the Pro Bowl. They made the playoffs in both seasons, and Glanville blossomed before our eyes into James Cagney.

One Sunday, he left tickets at will-call for Elvis Presley. When that gag got a few laughs, he followed up with freebies for James Dean, another of his heroes; the Phantom of the Opera, and other legends. He infuriated other coaches with his team's cheap shots. After one game, Chuck Noll of Pittsburgh met Glanville at midfield and wagged a finger in his face as he delivered a lecture on football decorum. By 1989, Cincinnati coach Sam Wyche, for one, had had enough.

The Oilers swaggered into Riverfront Stadium, known to the good burghers of Cincinnati as "the Jungle," needing one victory in their final two games to secure the first-ever outright division title since the AFL-NFL merger. Before their appearance, Glanville had derided Bengals fans, alleging they didn't "know how to boo." By the first quarter, with their team up 21-0, they were chanting, "Jer-ry, Jer-ry."

The Bengals didn't merely run over the Oilers, didn't merely run up the score, they brought out whips and chains and tire irons. With leads of 45 to 51 points, Wyche called for an onside kick, a cornerback blitz, a reverse, and a couple of fourth-down runs. With 21 seconds remaining, he ordered a field goal. But he had an explanation.

"He's probably the biggest phony in professional football," Wyche said of Glanville, "and I don't like people who are phonies. He's a liar. He tells me he didn't say things when I saw him say them on TV. And then, he comes and puts his arm around me. They've got the best talent in the AFC, possibly the league, but he brings them down. They play stupid football. We were going for their jugular and we weren't going to reset our heel, either.

"We don't like this team and we don't like their people. When you have a chance to do this, you do it. I wish the game was five quarters so we could have hit triple digits. What did they get, seven? I guess we had a little letdown. The Oilers just got embarrassed and humiliated and I would hate to ride that plane back home and play the Cleveland Browns the next week. The Browns won't quit. They're not that kind of people and I would hate to play them with that sorry team we saw on the field today."

Otherwise, Wyche was calm. While he didn't cover himself with glory in the annals of either football or mental hygiene, he probably earned a few "Attaboys" from other coaches. His quarterback, Boomer Esiason, employed the devil-made-us-do-it defense: "I feel bad about being like this, but they do bring out the worst in you."

A day later, Esiason called his friend Moon to explain. "Boomer just hated that I had to go through that," Moon reported, "because he likes me as a person and thinks I'm a pretty decent guy."

The next week, the Oilers lost to Cleveland at home. The following week, they lost to Chuck Noll's Steelers in the wild-card playoff in the Astrodome.

At home, Glanville visited sick kids in hospitals and looked for fights wherever he could find them. "He was always asking me to do things for him, personal things," said Joe Dugger, a police officer who held down a second job in the Oilers' locker room. "The first hundred times he asked, I did them, I swear, but then he wanted me to pick his kid up after school and take him to the doctor, and I had something I had to do and I couldn't. When I told him, he called me every name he could think of, names I hadn't heard before, and I thought I'd heard 'em all."

John McClain, who had covered the team for the *Houston Chronicle* since the Bum Phillips days with an even-handed grace, got a taste when Glanville called him out. Analyzing the situation quickly, McClain decided he'd lose whether he won or lost the fight and declined. Glanville's verbal sparring with the press reached comic proportions occasionally, as when he refused at a Monday press conference to answer one of my questions.

He had few friends in the media — he once called Bob Allen, sports anchor on the local ABC-TV affiliate "the little, short, fuzzy-head guy" — but Glanville had a particular aversion to some. I was one, possibly because I referred to him repeatedly in print as "Ladd's little bobo," borrowing from my time on the baseball beat in Chicago a term for a sycophant.

Each Monday after a game, Glanville had a press session scheduled at the team's practice facility at 12:30 p.m., after which the media were allowed into the locker to quiz players until 1:00. The problem was that Glanville usually arrived late and never pushed back the time at which the media had to clear the locker, leaving precious little time for interviews with players.

When I asked a question one week, Glanville barked, "I'm not answering your questions," at which point no one else said anything and the session broke up. The next week, I sat next to veteran broadcaster Barry Warner, who had stuck the "Bottom-Line Bud" tag on Adams years before. As time grew short, Warner leaned over and said, "You gonna ask a question?" I nodded. "Ask it now," he said, "so we can get out of here and get the players." I threw out some innocuous thing about the linebackers' play or something, Glanville refused to answer, the meeting broke up, and Warner slapped me a high-five.

Glanville never did figure out that his rooster strut often propelled him blindly into the other guys' hands. The Oilers became Public Enemy No. 1 on other teams' schedules, especially those of their division opponents. In 1987, they beat Seattle in overtime in a wild-card playoff game in the Astrodome and advanced to the divisional round in Denver.

The Broncos got the ball first, and Houston forced a punt. On first down from the five-yard line, a plunge into the middle lost a yard. On second down, the Oilers didn't huddle, instead lining up with tackles Bruce Davis and Dean Steinkuhler and tight end Jamie Williams spread far left of the rest of the formation and back Mike Rozier behind them.

Warren Moon took the snap, spun and threw an overhand lateral to Rozier, a good runner who could have adopted the nickname "Hands of Stone" if boxer Roberto Duran hadn't beaten him to it. The ball clanged off his mitts, the Broncos recovered at the one and scored for a 7-0 lead. After Denver wrapped up a 34-10 victory, Glanville did nothing to quiet the gales of laughter that had echoed through the press box, the stands, and America's living rooms all afternoon by declaring that he had christened the play "Stagger Lee."

In the NBC-TV booth, Dick Enberg and Merlin Olsen slogged through a tedious three hours by replaying the play repeatedly and marveling at how any coach could have called it in that situation. Obviously, they didn't know Glanville. He had pointed one gun at his head before arriving in the Rockies, declaring, "We're going to the

Super Bowl." The Broncos, defending AFC champions, took umbrage at that forecast and cinched up their chin straps a bit tighter. On his team's second play of the game, Glanville cocked another pistol and stuck it in his mouth.

In the aftermath, he insisted the play would have gained 30 yards if only Rozier had caught the ball. Whatever, the Denver staff punctuated the extent to which he was reviled around the league by revealing that Chuck Noll had tipped them off to the gadget play. It didn't show up in the exchange of films — each team was required to ship the other those of only its three previous games — but Glanville had called it earlier in the season against Pittsburgh.

As Denver prepared for the Oilers, Noll alerted the Broncos' coaches to Glanville's trick. The Oilers practiced it all week, but their players might have been more surprised than their opponents when the call came in as they scrimmaged from their four.

The country got a belly laugh at Houston's expense. As dusk settled on Mile High Stadium, an orange-clad Denver fan waved a banner reading, "Jerry, can I have your Super Bowl tickets?" And the Oilers wondered if they would ever be relieved of their sideshow responsibilities and allowed to express their considerable football talent.

"Next season," said Williams, the tight end, "we need to learn how not to self-destruct as a team. We still have to cut down on penalties. I think we've got the respect of other teams, so we don't need to beat guys up after the play."

I harbored a secret suspicion that, way down deep, Glanville didn't want to win a Super Bowl. The man was enraptured with the underdog identification he had created for himself — to all appearances,

he truly enjoyed the time he spent with critically ill kids in hospitals
— and would have been adrift in a black space suit in the role of
champion.

Some of his players bought his act as though it were stock in a
gold mine at a penny a share. Especially enamored were several special-teamers, who lacked the skills and job security of the starters. A
few defensive regulars jumped in as well, notably cornerback Cris
Dishman, who threatened to crack the FBI's Ten Most Wanted with
his serial atrocities. Almost to a man, the offensive starters smoul-
dered in silence at the lack of discipline on the team.

Glanville eventually became so caught up in his shtick that he
brought down the wrath of his father. A segment of the public was
swept up in his underdog routine, and the more positive feedback
Glanville got, the farther he pushed it. He liked to tell stories of his
deprived youth in the housing projects of Detroit, especially when a
writer for a national magazine pulled out his tape recorder. In Jerry's
version, his father abandoned the family and vanished when Jerry was
just a tyke. When his father, by this time living in Arizona, picked up
on the theme, he surfaced to say that while he and Jerry's mother had
divorced, he had provided support for years. He also filed a slander
action against his son.

By 1989, the Oilers had gone 19-12 over the previous two seasons, making the playoffs in each, and their talent level was obvious
to all. Herzeg's deep and abiding affection for Glanville had cooled
as the coach drew more and more attention to himself. Holovak had
won rave reviews for his drafting, but in '88 Herzeg had stripped
him of his VP title and banished him to Sarasota, Florida, as a glo-
rified scout.

In February, 1989, Herzeg resigned, and Adams brought Holovak
back as general manager, a poor choice. For all his success as a talent

appraiser, Holovak was not an administrator or negotiator. With Herzeg out of the way, however, Glanville was set to run to daylight. By this time, alas, the Oilers were expected to win, and win big.

It appeared they might do just that. By week 15, they stood 9-5 and had won five of their last six, including a victory over the hated Steelers in Pittsburgh. But then up jumped Sam Wyche and the Bengals to paste that 61-7 hickey on Glanville at Riverfront Stadium. The Browns came to the Astrodome and won the last game of the season and the Steelers followed with an overtime victory in the wild-card playoff round in Houston. Jerry's time was up.

At a press conference announcing his departure, he and Adams teared up and embraced, and the owner said Glanville was leaving by "mutual agreement." He got the head job in Atlanta, where Falcons owner Rankin Smith was desperate for an act that would sell tickets. Floyd Reese, one of Glanville's staff, first accepted the title of assistant head coach with the Falcons, then decided instead to take a front-office position with the Oilers. Glanville mailed him a black rose.

The NFL schedule-maker put the Oilers-Falcons grudge match first on the 1990 schedule. With his new troops frothing and the Oilers playing with what would become a characteristic tentativeness under Jack Pardee, Glanville won, 47-27. Then he said:

"Texas can kiss my butt."

LADD
TIDINGS

Meanwhile, Glanville's former rabbi, Herzeg, was by this time hiding out in his native Cleveland. He was finished with Houston, but Houston wasn't through with him.

A little girl wondered who her daddy was, and where he was. Her mother worked three jobs and wondered if she'd ever see a dime of child support. Joann DeNicola was a flight attendant working an Oilers charter when she met Herzeg, the roly-poly silver-tongued devil with a flair for dramatic entrances into people's lives.

With the team on a trip to Buffalo, he had become incensed at the noise raised by a wedding party at the team's hotel. When he didn't get the desired result by ordering them to tone it down, Herzeg dropped his pants and mooned the group. He also allegedly struck one of the guests. Police appeared and led the Oilers general manager off to jail in handcuffs. Charges were later dropped.

In another incident, charges were never filed. Herzeg made a weekly appearance during the football season on a radio show hosted by Barry Warner, who hailed from Buffalo. The two weren't exactly Lake Erie soulmates, but you couldn't tell it by their accents. Warner, who had done some pro football scouting before entering the media, regularly grilled his guest with questions beginning, "Ladd, why woun't you . . ." Herzeg would respond with, "Barry, we coun't do that because . . ." Their words assaulted a Texan's ear like rumors that oil had just dropped another nickel a barrel.

On one show, Herzeg complained of his treatment at the hands of two *Houston Chronicle* columnists, Fran Blinebury and me, adding, "At least I know Fowler. I've never even met Blinebury." Warner took it upon himself to arrange an introduction. The three convened for lunch at Tony's, an upscale eatery favored by the old-money crowd in River Oaks. Five hours later, all hell broke loose.

Herzeg immediately began ordering Cristal champagne at $145 a bottle. He and Blinebury went through five — Warner doesn't drink — and after cleaning out that section of the cellar dropped down to one bottle of a sprightly but unpretentious Dom Perignon at $105. By all accounts, Herzeg and Blinebury got on like old army buddies. Warner said when he left at midafternoon to do his show, those two were regaling each other with stories and slapping their knees. At about 4:30, by which time the restaurant had emptied of all patrons but them, Herzeg reached across the table and cuffed Blinebury twice, hard, on the side of the head. He then wobbled out of his chair and headed for the door.

Stunned, Blinebury remained long enough to pay the check of $1,066 — that did include tax and tip — and then followed Herzeg out, his nose dripping blood. The GM was seated in his top-of-the-line BMW, and as Blinebury, still unsure of his response, reached for the door handle, Herzeg squealed away into the January gloaming. In River Oaks, he wrecked his car. Police deposited him on Adams's nearby doorstep.

"Ladd better be glad it was the River Oaks police that found him and not the Houston police," Adams said later. "They would have taken him to jail. I drove him home that night and he was so [drunk] he couldn't remember where he lived."

While Herzeg got a lift home from his boss, Blinebury got his column suspended for several weeks by his paper. David Burgin, editor of the *Chronicle's* competitor, the *Houston Post*, got in the last word. A *Post* story concluded with this quote from him: "We urge *Post* sports columnists to order Dom Perignon '66, an exquisite vintage. It's more expensive ($800 a bottle), but it's a kinder, gentler champagne, far more cerebral and less likely to provoke a contretemps."

DeNicola might have shared a bottle of bubbly with Herzeg on the night she became pregnant by him. If so, her hangover lasted much longer than Blinebury's.

In the salad days, the tomato was in rapture. DeNicola said after he vanished that they had lived together for several years while he was still married to Kathy Herzeg, whom he had met and wed in Cleveland before moving to Houston. After Meghan came along, Herzeg never tried to hide his paternity. On the contrary, he wore it like a campaign ribbon. He took the infant to games at the Astrodome and invited the media into his private box to photograph them together. He hoisted her on his shoulders and walked from end zone to end zone before a game, posing for more pictures.

Three days after the team lost a January 1, 1989, playoff game, Herzeg told an interviewer in his office, "In years past, after a loss like

we had in Buffalo, a normal day for me would have been watching the
game film over and over, replaying the whole game in my mind. But
what I did on Monday was pick up my daughter, have brunch with
her, play with her, put her down for a nap, change her. She has given
me a different outlook on life. It's easier to go to work. Now, I can
read a critical column, then I look at Meghan's picture and I don't give
the criticism a second thought."

He broke into sobs during the interview and concluded, pointing
to three pictures of his child, "How can you get upset when you've got
something as wonderful as this?"

Less than a month later, he quit his $450,000-a-year job and left
town, not to see his daughter again for years, if ever.

"Ladd actually walked out on me," said Adams. "In the end, I
guess he thought he had me over a barrel. He had picked Mike
Holovak's brain and he was pushing Mike out. He walked in here and
said he wanted a raise to $750,000. I told him I'd give him $500,000
and put him on probation for a year. I told him he already had three
strikes with Blinebury, the gal (DeNicola), etc., but he walked out."

Herzeg didn't forget his child, at least not immediately. At Easter
in her fifth year, she received from him in the mail a present of puffed
letters for learning the alphabet — they cost $55; the price tag was
included — and four bags of candy. He had no way of knowing that
Meghan already knew her letters. On Mother's Day, DeNicola
received a card from a golf resort in Tennessee. Herzeg also sent a
scorecard and a note to Meghan: "Your (maternal) granddaddy would
love to play this course."

DeNicola had received postcards from other golf resorts, and the
child received cards from Disney World, Rome, London, Paris, Monte
Carlo, and Hungary. In a letter, he told DeNicola he mailed cards to
her as he roamed the globe "to inflict pain," knowing she loved to

Bud Adams (right) and Roy Hofheinz with the Astrodome, over which they split.

The flirtation that fizzled: Jacksonville mayor Tommy Hazouri tries on Bud Adams's cowboy hat.

Oh, and while the woo is on, Bud gets a tour of Jacksonville's football stadium.

Warren Moon can't stand to watch.

A happier scenario: Moon looking to go long.

Head coach Jerry Glanville with his buddy, Elvis.

Glanville (left) and GM Ladd Herzeg, comrades forever?

Herzeg holds daughter Meghan, the only way he ever supported her.

Bud and Jerry say a soggy goodbye.

Jack Pardee, who replaced Glanville, was often puzzled.

Another tough day at the office for quarterback Moon.

Earl Campbell tramples the Chicago Bears.

Bum Phillips, overwhelmed by fans' show of support after a playoff loss in Pittsburgh.

Phillips and former QB Dan Pastorini reliving "Luv Ya Blue!" memories.

Former GM and coach Sid Gillman (left) and longtime Oilers center Carl Mauck at a dinner honoring Bum in 1980.

Sir Bud Adams, in ascot, surveys his domain.

Nashville mayor Phil Bredesen gets a jersey from Bud, along with the image overhaul.
(AP Photo/Mark Humphrey)

Parting is such sweet sorrow. (AP Photo/David J. Phillip)

travel. Herzeg also sent Meghan a vanity magazine cover — a photo made to appear that he had posed for the cover of *Ski*.

"I'm working three jobs and this man is playing golf," DeNicola said. "He still refers to Meghan as his daughter, but he has no idea. We could be living under [a bridge] for all he knows. I did what I did, and I don't feel I'm paying a price or anything. The loss is his because he doesn't know what a beautiful child we have."

A judge ordered Herzeg to pay $84,000 in back child support, plus interest and attorneys' fees that brought the total to $150,000. Because he was unemployed, the court could not attach his wages. The district attorney's office declined to go to the expense of having him forcibly returned to Texas. DeNicola's lawyer sent out more than 1,000 posters offering a $500 reward for information on his where-abouts, and the NBC-TV program "Prime Suspect" ran a story seeking to flush him out. Herzeg remained hidden.

The man who once promised to marry DeNicola and have "a tribe of children" with her sent a five-page letter to the *Chronicle* accusing her of greed and of using their daughter as a pawn. He contended she turned down an offer of $1,500 a month in support payments and an equal sum paid into a trust fund for the child. "Some day," he wrote, "Ms. DeNicola and I will be judged not by the judicial system and not by the court of public opinion, but by our daughter when she is old enough."

After the child was born, Herzeg and his wife divorced in what DeNicola's lawyer and others believed was a ploy to shield his assets from his flesh and blood. In a deposition taken after DeNicola filed a conspiracy suit against the two, Kathy Herzeg admitted she received an "overwhelmingly favorable" settlement that included $212,000 in cash, real estate, securities, insurance policies, and rights to her ex-husband's pension and retirement benefits. She maintained Herzeg provided for her so generously out of guilt over his affair with DeNicola.

"I love Ladd; that's why I had his child," said DeNicola. "It wasn't a one-nighter. We were together, lived together, for years before anyone in the media knew about it. Now, he thinks I turned on him. He never thought I'd get a court order [severing his parental rights] and his ego can't stand it. That's why he sends me these cards from golf resorts, rubbing my nose in it.

"He was a monster at the end."

Said Adams: "As for Ladd, he was a hard-nosed bean counter. He was smart and he was good at negotiating with the players. He did a good job, and I put a lot of faith in him. When he really let me down was when the pressure started getting to him, which I didn't realize at first."

After Ladd and Kathy divorced, I went to Philadelphia on an Oilers trip and stayed at the team hotel. On the Saturday night before the game, I arranged to meet two friends in the bar and arrived first. I ordered a drink, and shortly the waitress brought another, saying, "The gentleman over there sent this one." I looked over my shoulder and peered through the smoky dark, spying Ladd and Kathy sitting in a booth with Rick Nichols, Herzeg's chief lieutenant, across from them. With no option but to retaliate, I sent three drinks to their table.

One of my friends had joined me when Herzeg walked over, carrying the three glasses. "Here, Ed," he said, setting them down on the table, "you'd better take these back. I've got to get Kathy out of here before she throws them on you." The three of them left the bar.

Some time after Herzeg left the Oilers, a caller to my radio show reported a Ladd sighting at an airport in West Virginia. In line at a rental car counter, he recognized the fellow in front of him despite a change in hair color and leaned over for a glance at his driver's license to make sure. "Ladd had bleached his hair blond," the caller related, "and he had two black eyes and he had a sleazy-looking blonde with him."

That description did not fit Kathy.

No one questioned Herzeg's mind. In retrospect, he even appears prescient. In 1982, the year the Raiders moved from Oakland to Los Angeles, he wrote a guest column for the *Chronicle* arguing for a limited exemption from antitrust laws for the NFL. Herzeg made the case that the exemption would eliminate willy-nilly franchise shifting:

"Do you think there would have been support from businesses and fans [in Oakland] if everyone had been told the Raiders would pick up and leave when a better offer came along?

"Without this limited exemption from antitrust, the problem could come up over and over again in other league cities. The greed factor is there, and any owner could be vulnerable.

"If his community has supported the team for many years but attendance drops off when the team has two or three bad seasons, another city could put an unbelievable deal together.

"It might be a package similar to this:

"A group in Birmingham wants to bring the Houston Oilers or any other NFL team to that city. Business leaders in Birmingham write a letter of credit indicating that if the 70,000-seat stadium isn't sold out for every game over the next 10 years, they will draw from that letter to make up the difference. They promise to build a complete training facility. They guarantee the owner lower taxes for the next 20 years. They offer a sweetheart stadium lease for the next 30 years.

"From an economic standpoint, that would be a difficult offer to turn down. The only reasons for not moving would be moralistic. But if the NFL gets its limited exemption from antitrust law, the owner would not be permitted to move if the people in his community have supported the team through the years.

"The partial exemption would protect loyal fans from human nature, if the owner happens to be greedy . . .

"Losing a franchise can cost a community money, but it hurts in other ways. A large segment of society feels great Monday morning if their NFL team won the day before. They're even buzzing if the team loses.

"Those people who follow the team are much more interested in reading about their team than about Exxon's third-quarter earnings report. Is it fair to take a team away from those people just because some other city made a better deal?"

10

"To Oiler," Verb, Transitive

The Houston Oilers and the English language both took a beating on January 3, 1993, Bud Adams's 70th birthday. The Oilers were . . . well, there we go, groping for adjectives again. The word was not "devastated."

"I think we need to have another word placed into the English dictionary to describe this loss," said cornerback Cris Dishman, "because it goes beyond 'devastated.' It was the biggest choke in history. We choked. We choked as a team, we choked as an organization. We got outplayed and outcoached."

Well, he tried. Suffice it to say, the 41-38 overtime loss to the Bills in Buffalo marked the greatest collapse in the 73-year history of the National Football League. Houston had led 35-3 early in the third quarter. No other team has ever expectorated a lead of as many as 32 points. It was Oileresque.

In the aftermath, golfers who left a putt short grimaced and spat,

"I Oilered it." People far from Houston experienced a need to get their feelings out. David Letterman shared with the nation the Top 10 Oilers Excuses:

10. Shouldn't have skipped breakfast. It's the most important meal of the day.
9. Started giving 109 percent instead of 110 percent.
8. Even though fans loved it, shouldn't have replaced Warren Moon with folk singer Suzanne Vega.
7. Busy making mental tally of football players with girls' names: Fran Tarkenton, Rosie Grier . . .
6. You try tackling those guys. Some of them are huge.
5. Bills QB kept looking one way, then throwing the other.
4. Wanted to honor another Houstonian (President George Bush) who let a big lead in the polls slip away.
3. "I'm telling you . . . Maybe you didn't see the Dobermans on the field, but there were Dobermans on the field!"
2. Preoccupied about getting home in time to see all the Amy Fisher movies.
1. Didn't want to go to Disney World.

In my column in the *Chronicle*, I appealed to the poet Robert Service for the right words:

Then on a sudden the music changed,
so soft that you scarce could hear;
But you felt that your life had been looted clean of all
that it once held dear;
That someone had stolen the woman you loved;
that her love was a devil's lie;
That your guts were gone,
and the best for you was to crawl away and die . . .

But the Oilers weren't getting off that easy.

For weeks after the playoff loss in Buffalo, Bud Adams kept the profile of a grass snake. General manager Mike Holovak announced the firing of defensive coordinator Jim Eddy and secondary coach Pat Thomas. It wasn't unusual for Bud to drop out of public view for long stretches, but fans clamored for information, and blood. Only Adams could address the fate of Holovak and coach Jack Pardee, and the owner could have been in Tibet for all anyone knew. A rumor circulated to the effect that he had locked himself in the bathroom in Rich Stadium and refused to come out. I know. I started it.

If not for his history, Bud might have emerged in this case as a sympathetic figure. After Jerry Glanville, the city ached for a man who would coach football and shut up. Adams was known to have a relationship with Jackie Sherrill, who was steering Texas A&M on a course for the jagged shoals of the NCAA's enforcement apparatus, and some feared Adams would hire his pal and invite more turmoil.

But even closer to home, Pardee was running up glitzy scores with his run-and-shoot offense at the University of Houston. What's more, he was a former NFL Coach of the Year and had taken both the Chicago Bears and Washington Redskins to the playoffs. For once, Adams made the popular move, handing the avuncular Pardee a five-year contract.

A Texan and a former All-America linebacker at A&M who had starred in the pros for the Los Angeles Rams, Pardee provided a greater contrast to Glanville than Jacqueline Onassis to Phyllis Diller. A man of erect bearing and deeply submerged emotions, Pardee discharged the public functions of his job with grace but no appetite.

A recent arrival from Borneo would have grasped immediately

that this was a man whose idea of a good time was sitting at home talking quietly with his wife or fishing off the pier in his back yard. Pardee had been a vicious hitter as a player, but you would hand over a new-born babe into his arms without a second thought. He had beaten cancer, but a crowbar was required to get more than a cursory comment out of him on any aspect of his life.

Jack was the anti-Jerry, and that suited Houston just fine — in terms of style. His football team was another matter. Pardee took over a team that had made the playoffs the previous three years. In his four full seasons, the Oilers played into the tournament each year. Over the seven-year span, the Oilers were the only team in the league to crack postseason play in each. Their playoff record under Pardee was 1-4.

A blood-and-guts player himself, Pardee had embraced the run-and-shoot offense, a kinky four-wide-receiver set with one running back that relied heavily on precision timing between quarterback and pass-catcher. It had served him well at the University of Houston, which labored under a recruiting disadvantage vis-a-vis Texas and Texas A&M. The run-and-shoot employed athletes the other schools didn't want, usually because they were undersized.

Glanville had used a similar set with the Oilers, one he called the Red Gun, and other NFL teams used it as he did — as a complement to the base offense. Pardee put his team in the run-and-shoot and never pulled it out.

Like Glanville before him, Pardee faced high expectations. In 1988, Glanville's penultimate year, the Oilers sent eight men to the Pro Bowl. In Pardee's four seasons, they never sent fewer than six and once as many as nine. The talent level was undeniable. Fans expected a team with that many stud buzzards to bust through into the Super Bowl.

As the Oilers bombed each January, the run-and-shoot came increasingly under attack. A couple of other teams tried it as a staple offense and discarded it. If no one else wanted it, it must be an orphan offense, mustn't it? Pardee and offensive coordinator Kevin Gilbride stuck by their system although Gilbride occasionally pointed out that he could coach others as well, as though to indicate the run-and-shoot was Pardee's baby, not his.

Warren Moon rang up staggering yardage totals, but scoring efficiency didn't keep pace as the offense sputtered in the red zone, from the opponents' 20-yard line to the goal. On a shortened field, defenses jammed the receivers on the line and swarmed to the ball in the secondary. With only five blockers and one runner, the Oilers could rely on neither brute strength nor the element of surprise when a running play was indicated. Running time off the clock with a ground attack to protect a lead had also proved a problem.

Still, when a team is cracking the playoffs on an annual basis, the thinkers are loathe to tinker with the system. Gilbride came under withering fire on the talk shows each time the Oilers came acropper in the postseason, and Pardee let him. Not once did the head coach step up and say, "I decide what system we use and the coordinator implements it." Gilbride, who would move on to Jacksonville and oversee the offense on a team that made the playoffs in its second year of existence and then to San Diego as head coach, was Houston's favorite whipping boy.

What he couldn't say was that the formation never dropped a pass. In 1991, Pardee's second year, the Oilers won 11 of 16 games and beat the New York Jets in a wild-card game in the Astrodome. They headed for Denver next, and all week fans studied the weather forecast like the Dead Sea Scrolls. In addition to its other limitations, the run-and-shoot was regarded as a poor foul-weather offense because of its heavy reliance on passing. Moon, with all those years in Canada behind him, had thrown accurately enough in cold and wet conditions, but he couldn't tame the wind.

Instead of a blizzard, the Oilers and Broncos drew a mild day for January on the Front Porch of the Rockies. Moon couldn't miss early. He hit Haywood Jeffires and Drew Hill for scores as Houston broke on top, 14-0. The Broncos got one touchdown back but missed the kick. Moon found Curtis Duncan for another touchdown to put the Oilers up, 21-6. Denver countered before the half and added a field goal in the third quarter. Still, when Al Del Greco knocked in a chip shot for three, Houston led, 24-16, in the final quarter.

An archivist would probably trace the reason for the Oilers' loss on that day to the presence of one John Elway on the other side. The Denver passer had made a career of miracle comebacks the way others spend their lives running a drill press. It was almost ho-hum as he whipped the Broncos to a touchdown and then passed them into position for a decisive field goal, a 28-yarder by Jeff Treadwell, as the Houston defense went into helter-skelter mode.

Statistics would show that Moon passed for 325 yards with three touchdowns and one interception. Elway threw for 257 yards with one touchdown and one interception. Denver won.

At the autopsy, the run-and-shoot was again fingered as the culprit. As the Broncos meandered downfield to the clinching points, the Houston defense could neither put consistent pressure on Elway nor maintain coverage on his receivers. And while it's true the Oilers scored just three points in the second half, Moon spied an open Jeffires in the end zone and delivered a laser strike to his numbers. Jeffires dropped the ball. He might have run out of the pro set, the wishbone, or the single wing, but he had lined up in the run-and-shoot, so the run-and-shoot must have been the problem.

For a team that hasn't won so much as its conference championship since the merger of the two leagues, history is never an ally. Just as the ghost of Stagger Lee had boarded the plane with the Oilers as they shipped out to Denver for that playoff game in January, 1992, their trip to Buffalo a year later brought back memories of a postseason loss at Rich Stadium during the Glanville era, to say nothing of Herzeg's moon shot.

The more recent past was far kinder. The Oilers had closed the '92 season with four victories in their last five games, including a 27-3 pasting of the Bills in the Astrodome in the final game. At 10-6, they hadn't lived up to their billing as a consensus choice to make the Super Bowl, but they had secured another wild card to remain in the running.

When they pranced off the field at halftime with a 28-3 lead, they looked like a lock. The Bills played without four injured starters, including quarterback Jim Kelly and linebacker Cornelius Bennett, and lost star running back Thurman Thomas in the second quarter. Moon scored almost at will, hitting Haywood Jeffires twice and Webster Slaughter and Curtis Duncan for touchdowns. No team had ever blown a lead of more than 28 points and lost, and the Oilers were up by 25.

In the press box at halftime, several members of the Houston media jumped on the phone to make travel arrangements for the following weekend. The only cautionary note came from O.J. Simpson, best known at the time as a former Bills great and a fellow who sprinted through airports in commercials. Pulling duty as a sideline reporter for television, he ducked into the press box at the half to warm up and said, "If any team could blow it, it would be Houston."

In the locker, Moon thought back not to the dissection of the Bills a week earlier but to the game one year before at Mile High Stadium. "The first thing I said was, 'Remember Denver last year? Don't let it happen again.'"

He knew the Oilers.

The third quarter had scarcely begun before a thinned-out crowd well short of the 75,141 who had paid their way in when safety Bubba McDowell ripped off a pass and returned the ball 58 yards for a score that put Houston up by 35-3. On the Buffalo sideline, coach Marv Levy never changed expression, but then Levy's face was in a deep freeze in August. Huddled in his parka, Levy watched his breath freeze and plotted ways to put his Ph.D. to use. His team clearly couldn't outplay the Oilers, so perhaps he could out-think them.

That would prove only a modest challenge.

"Did I think we still had a chance?" Levy would say. "Well, there was a lot of time left, so there was a glimmer of hope, but it was about the same chance as you have of winning the New York Lottery."

Against any other team, perhaps less. Against the Oilers, the Bills actually took the lead in the fourth quarter. Suicide in Buffalo was once deemed redundant, but the Oilers' act was as noisome as hazardous waste. They had left their toxic spoor elsewhere around this great nation of ours, but in Buffalo they outdid themselves. It was Oileresque.

Frank Reich had made a good living for a part-time employe. In eight seasons as Buffalo's backup quarterback, he had made six previous starts. A television producer casting a fellow to glide along the sideline under a baseball cap while carrying a clipboard would have thought of him immediately. At the University of Maryland, he had brought the Terrapins back from a 31-0 halftime deficit to beat Miami, with Bernie Kosar at quarterback, 42-40, at the Orange Bowl. But that had been eight languorous seasons before.

If he felt any pressure at his summons to duty in a playoff game, it had eased by the third quarter. "When it's 35-3," he said, "you don't really feel a lot of pressure." He had the Oilers right where he wanted them.

Levy explained his man's four-touchdown second half in terms of his faith. "Frank is a person of high character," the philosopher-coach said. "He's a well-rounded family man who is deeply religious. Sometimes, the guy who has other things in his life doesn't clutch up. It makes him able to retain an equilibrium."

If that's the case, Jack Pardee should have gone to church. Or a synagogue, a mosque, a hobby shop, a knitting class. Football was his life, and his life as an NFL coach was almost at an end.

The Bills didn't do anything fancy in that second half. Their receivers simply aimed the hard-charging bison on their helmets at the seams in the Houston zone, caught Reich's passes, and ran across the goal line. Their only trick was an onside kick after their first touchdown, which caught the Oilers so unawares that the kicker, Steve Christie, recovered.

Kenneth Davis scored that first touchdown on a one-yard run, and then Reich hit Don Beebe for six and Andre Reed for six and six again. The 28 points was the highest total in a quarter in the history of the NFL playoffs. As the final period opened, Reed was still larking about the Houston secondary like a stray note. Reich found him for a third touchdown, and the Oilers, who had outscored the Bills by 62-6 in little more than six consecutive quarters, now had been outpointed by 35-0 in about one quarter. The 28-point third-quarter orgy consumed less than seven minutes.

Houston trailed by three.

The Oilers were not without guilt in terms of execution. Punter Greg Montgomery muffed a punt just 25 yards, Moon threw an interception, Montgomery bobbled the snap on a field-goal attempt. Still, allowing a cushion that deep to deflate requires a massive flaw in design. The Oilers deployed their defense in a soft zone for the second half and remained in it even as Reed and Beebe carved it up on the same few basic plays. On the sideline, Pardee was a picture of paralysis.

"We played a lot more man[-to-man] defense in the first half," said Dishman, the cornerback. "Then we went to a softer zone with the big lead. Then they made some adjustments while we stuck to our same coverages. We knew they were going to feature Andre Reed in the second half, but we stayed in the same zones. When you play the same things all the time, teams are going to beat you. It was the same old coverage."

The Oilers finally maneuvered close enough for Del Greco to kick a 26-yard field goal with 12 seconds to play that forced an overtime period. Houston won the toss and got the ball, but on the third play Nate Odomes intercepted a Moon pass at the Oilers' 37. Two plays later, Christie lined up a 32-yarder. On NBC-TV, Charlie Jones had the call: "It is right . . . down . . . the middle. And the celebration begins in Buffalo."

Celebration? It's a fair guess Buffalonians drank the town dry of Genessee that night, after their Bills spoiled Bud's birthday. Adams left the stadium at the end of regulation, escaping the postgame hordes of interviewers. His players were not so lucky. "It's like somebody somewhere has a voodoo doll," said Ernest Givins, the wide receiver, "and when the Houston Oilers go on the road to play a playoff game, they start sticking pins in the voodoo doll until there's nothing left of the Houston Oilers."

Most of his teammates steered clear of the occult as they groped for the proper responses. Contrition was the theme of the day.

"When we had them down," said Dishman, "we should have cut their throats, but we let them breathe and gave them new life. Never in my wildest nightmares did I believe something like this could happen, but when they got that last interception in overtime and I saw their field position, I thought, 'Well, the Houston Oilers choked again.'"

Defensive end Sean Jones: "I wouldn't blame the fans if they never bought another ticket. To do what we just did is unthinkable. I'm not even mad right now."

Wide receiver Jeffires: "I can't blame Mr. Holovak if he wants to get rid of all of us."

Defensive end William Fuller: "I thought when we were eliminated from the playoffs last year at Denver it would be the low point of my career, but this is worse. This is the lowest ever."

Quarterback Moon: "I've never seen or experienced anything like that before. We had control of the ballgame like no team ever had control of a ballgame. Then for me to throw the pick in overtime that caused us to lose . . . I feel doubly rotten."

Their contempt for themselves was trifling compared to what the folks back home felt for them. One ex-fan piled a mound of memorabilia collected over decades in the street in front of his house and set it ablaze. Sports bar owners reported their establishments had been left in shambles — as well as empty five minutes after the game ended. Callers burned up the wires to sports talk shows, and the host of a current-events talker who had never allowed sports to creep into his show could discuss nothing else for the full three hours on the morning after.

"Some people were totally out of control with their anger and frustration," he said. "I have never seen anything like this."

It didn't help that the nation was cackling at Houston. In addition to Letterman, Arsenio Hall and Jay Leno took their shots. Rush Limbaugh even got into the act, playing the Oilers' fight song first at high volume and then at a barely audible level to simulate the team's performance dropoff. On CBS Hispanic Radio, listeners learned the Oilers had "no *corazon*."

Outgoing president George Bush invoked the name of the team in a speech at the U.S. Military Academy at West Point. "I guess the moral of all this is that losing is never easy. Trust me, I know something about that. But if you have to lose, fight with all you have, give it your best shot, and, win or lose, learn from it and get on with life." Bush was unquestionably sympathetic, but we must hope the cadets took his words to heart because no one back home did.

We can but wonder today at what shape the lampooning would have taken if the team had then been installed in Tennessee, but here's a wild stab: "Hee-Haw" would have come up.

A University of Houston sociologist, Bill Simon, said the city would somehow pull through. "Given our commitment to sports and the repeated failures of all three teams [Oilers, Astros, Rockets]," he said, "we have here a cumulative effect. It is that wonderful way of venting a whole series of emotions. Three days down the road, we all will feel slightly better."

Then he retreated again behind the ivy-covered walls and fans continued to bray. Holovak's firing of Eddy and Thomas on the day after hardly sated the blood lust. For many, only Pardee's head on a spike would have succeeded. Moon cleaned out his locker on Monday and slipped out a back door of the training facility to elude the media. When some cameras caught up with him anyway, he covered his face with a notebook, climbed into his car, and drove away.

Adams went into hiding and, it was later revealed, gave brief consideration to canning Pardee and his entire staff. He didn't dwell on the thought. The head coach had two years left on his contract at $500,000 annually. At the behest of the owner and general manager, Pardee let go two men who had been with him for almost 10 years, from the Houston Gamblers of the defunct United States Football League to the University of Houston to the Oilers. "I'd rather take a beating than have to tell them," he said. "It's times like these when you'd rather be selling insurance."

Except for the pay, he might as well have been. From that day forward, he was the head coach in title only.

The Oilers' problems, as ever, were organizational. Herzeg's iron fist had been replaced by a hand here and a hand there. Holovak held sway on the football side, but only on talent decisions. Negotiating contracts and running a staff were never his fortes, and Steve Underwood, for years a trusted attorney on Adams's staff, took over some of Herzeg's former functions. McClure had the boss's ear on business matters but he had to fend off a rival, Scott Thompson — like Herzeg, an accountant — who would stage a brief but spirited play for a seat in the inner sanctum.

Herzeg had controlled access to Adams, meaning, in effect, that no one else had any, but now everyone got an audience and everyone had an opinion.

Holovak and Pardee tolerated one another, but over the three years they had worked together the general manager had developed the opinion that the coach wasn't getting the most out of the talent provided him. It wasn't without foundation. Pardee, for all his fire as a player, could never get a spark going as a coach. He worked in a vacuum.

He had a habit of constantly washing one big hand over the back of the other, and on the sideline in Buffalo he had stood with arms folded throughout the second half as the Bills poured through his defense like the Germans through the Maginot Line. Pardee delegated not just authority but control to his coordinators, and he wouldn't intervene if the Panzers were blowing up his locker room.

When results began to deteriorate, Pardee would on rare occasions puff out his chest and deliver a gruff talk to the assembled players. This tactic produced the predictable result, none. He would not take problem children aside for what the Alabama boys call "a little prayer meetin'." Holovak tried to assume that role, but he was a man of the old school who knew only the frontal approach. With most of the young players, it worked no better than Pardee's classroom dressings-down. At one practice, Dishman was bumped on a play and began removing his pads, a signal that he was injured and couldn't continue. When Holovak reproached him, Dishman screamed obscenities at him, ending with, "Go to hell."

Players disposed to taking advantage of a meltdown at the top did just that. Ray Childress, the Pro Bowl defensive lineman who was normally a tight-lipped sort, went public with a charge of a lack of discipline. Challenged, the team lost its next game. Penalties continued to mount out of control, but for that Adams had an explanation. The owner said the Glanville influence hadn't been completely purged.

Matters were in a state of disarray, but we hadn't seen anything yet. Buddy Ryan was coming to town.

Holovak hired Ryan as defensive coordinator and instructed him to report directly to him. If the team had no *corazon*, Pardee proved he had no *cojones* when he abided this arrangement. Bud Quixote jumped into the fix-up act as well. The owner had become obsessed with an offensive coordinator when Phillips was his coach. When Bum refused to name one, Adams cited that as his reason for firing him.

When he and Glanville parted ways by "mutual agreement," he said Glanville's insistence on not naming a coordinator for either offense or defense had never been an issue between them. Pardee had coordinators, so Bud ordered him to find a tight end. The Oilers had blown a 32-point lead in less than two quarters in Buffalo, so the run-and-shoot must have been the culprit.

Buddy Ryan agreed. Oh, but did he agree.

11

OFFENSIVE DEFENSIVE COORDINATOR

Birth, death, charity, and Jerry Glanville are all gripping topics, at least when put into an Oilers context, and so it was that Buddy Ryan was forced to exercise every bit of his considerable flair for the theatrical to command attention in a 1993 football season scripted by Lewis Carroll. Jimmy Johnson peered down from his perch in Dallas and mused, "They should turn that thing into a soap opera down there. It would rate high in the Nielsen ratings."

Coming off the Oileresque effort in Buffalo, Jack Pardee didn't need added pressure, but no one was too concerned with what Pardee did or didn't need. Ryan hit town proclaiming that if the club would get linebacker Wilber Marshall for him, this would be a Super Bowl year. The Oilers acquired Marshall after Commissioner Paul Tagliabue ruled in their favor in a dispute with the Washington Redskins.

Then Bud Adams reported to training camp with the rookies for the first time since the inaugural season of the franchise, 1960, and declared, "I'll be the most surprised guy around if we don't at least get to the AFC championship game. I think we can win the AFC. We have great talent. We have the talent to get to the Super Bowl."

Nothing new there. What made Bud think the best talent would prevail this time only he knows, but his team would have, if it had nothing else, a chance for redemption in Buffalo. The Oilers played the Bills in their fifth game. By then, of course, things were in a fine mess. When he was head coach of the Philadelphia Eagles, Ryan had dubbed the run-and-shoot the "chuck-and-duck." Joining a team that employed the offense was scarcely enough reason to soften his stance. Ryan explained it would be hypocritical of him to change his assessment. And biting his tongue was never in the repertoire of a man who so thrived on confrontation that he cultivated it on every team he ever served.

As the curtain rose, Buddy was sniping away and the locker room was dividing into two armed camps. After a loss to New Orleans in the opener, Ryan second-guessed decisions by Pardee and Gilbride, put the blame on the offense, and fired on the run-and-shoot again. Ernest Givins appointed himself defender of the faith.

"Everybody wants to be a chief and call the shots," he said, "but there's only one man who should call the shots and that's Jack Pardee. Other guys are riled up but they're just not saying anything. I'm tired of hearing the same old bull."

Ryan's retort upon hearing Givins' comment: "I don't even know who he is."

He was one of the run-and-shoot's smurf receivers, and Ryan might have been exaggerating only slightly. He routinely forgot the names of players even on his defense, if he ever knew them, and called those men by their jersey numbers. By the time they arrived in Buffalo, the scene of so many glorious moments in the annals of the franchise, the Oilers stood 1-3.

"I'm depressed right now," Bud belched. "Something's wrong, but I can't put my finger on it." Unable to pinpoint the problem, he lashed out at players who invested too much of their time in charity work. "They have to get their off-field commitments off their backs so we can start playing football," he ordained. "Some of them have too many activities they're doing. It's fine for charity functions and all that but, my gosh, these guys are getting paid enough so they can spend all their time on football. They can do all the charity things they want to do when the season's over. They have too many functions going on. They need to be thinking football."

Warren Moon, probably the player most active in various causes, noted that he wasn't any more involved in those activities than in the past, and Bud let the matter drop. If his tirade dissolved his depression for the moment, it returned in a flood when his do-gooders let their bleeding hearts fall out and onto the Rich Stadium turf.

A 35-7 loss dropped them another notch. So much for redemption, but fortunately the owner kept his pudgy finger to himself thereafter. His team would not lose again in the regular season. Such a statement should not be misconstrued to mean the Oilers were wondrously transformed into one of those happy sports cliches and harmony and brotherhood prevailed. This was Bud's club, and even the birth of a child could prove a mixed blessing.

Debi Williams never wanted to be a celebrity, only a mom. Her easygoing husband, David, played right tackle for the Oilers, and played the position well. Nine months earlier — who knows, a starry night, a bottle of wine, a particular movie? — they weren't thinking football. It would have been just after the season ended with the spectacular choke in Buffalo, and so they were within their rights, even by Bud's rules.

Charity began at home that evening, and little Scot Cooper Williams was the result. Heedless of the views of his father's boss on distractions during the season, he popped into the world on the eve of the 1-4 Oilers' momentous date with the New England Patriots in Foxboro, Massachusetts. When he did, Mom should have ordered extra diapers for the Oilers organization.

If Babygate didn't rock the nation, it sent out a tremor felt in the Northeast. At the World Series at the time, I read about it in the Toronto, Philadelphia, and New York papers. I heard about it on television. Doing my radio show over the phone with my partner, John O'Reilly, in Houston, I discussed nothing but baby Scot for a week. The Fall Classic had been upstaged by a 9-pound, 15-ounce bundle of joy, and by Bud, who was sucking his thumb.

Even with Glanville far away, the Oilers cooked up a large order of machos deluxe when Williams skipped the game to remain with his wife after she gave birth. Offensive coordinator Kevin Gilbride and line coach Bob Young chastised their tackle, with Young comparing the situation to World War II, when many men went off to defend democracy, leaving pregnant wives at home. Pardee felt strongly both ways, but Bud added the jalapenos on top. Docking Williams a week's pay, $111,111, he gurgled, "Hear me on this: no play, no pay."

The proud parents turned down more than 70 media requests, honoring only one from "Eye to Eye With Connie Chung." When Scot took a snooze, his father clearly wanted to let a sleeping baby lie. "I did everything I could to try to get there," Williams said, "but now I just want to forget about it and get on with the season. I hope the

Oilers don't have any hard feelings. I know I don't." He termed the fine "money well spent."

Bud, however, developed colic. Noting that the child arrived 17 1/2 hours before kickoff, the owner insisted Williams had not made a good-faith effort to reach Foxboro in time for the game. "He could have gotten on an airplane," Bud raged. "The man makes $2 million a year; he ought to be able to make other arrangements. He's capable of doing what he needs to do. He thought $11,700 (the cost of a chartered flight) was too much money. Some of his teammates had offered to pay part of it, but he turned it down."

Williams denied spurning any such offer. He did note that Oilers officials had called the delivery room so many times before the birth that a doctor ripped the phone off the wall. "I don't believe that," Bud said. "Have you ever been in a delivery room? There's no phones in a delivery room." Williams just chuckled. "Well, I can get six or seven doctors and nurses to verify that," he said, "but I would rather put it all behind me."

The man who would ride to the rescue of Nashville's image had the final say. "It was great publicity," Bud sang. "It's not often that Houston gets on the map like that."

Even without Williams, the Oilers defeated the Patriots, the first of 11 consecutive victories, the longest winning streak in the league since the undefeated 1973 Miami Dolphins. At 12-4, they tied Buffalo and Dallas for best record in the NFL and sent eight men to the Pro Bowl. They put four players on the All-Pro first team and two more on the second team. Just as Bud had said, his team had the best talent in the conference.

Ryan's men picked up his "46" defense and cold-cocked the

league, allowing only one team to score more than 17 points in that 11-game run to glory. Boogaloo Bud jiggled in his suite, glass in hand, as his worthies defeated each division foe at home. They beat them all on the road as well, and whipped the 49ers at Candlestick Park on Christmas Day. Included in the run was a 33-17 flaying of Atlanta in the Astrodome. The Oilers had paid back Jerry Glanville.

"It was almost like watching us play back in 1988," Moon said. "That razzing stuff they did was a lot like what we used to do when Jerry was here, but we realized that his teams tend to self-destruct in close games on the road. That's what we used to do, and that's what they did today. There's no love lost between us, believe me. This is one of the most satisfying victories for me. I downplayed it all week but this is a game I really wanted."

Even some of Glanville's former defensive players reveled in the triumph. "He's so predictable," said end Sean Jones. "You don't have to be a psych major to figure him out. He wants to get you off your game plan with fights and intimidation. Once he realized he couldn't do it to us and he actually had to coach to beat us, he messed it up. The only two bad years I ever had in this league was when that . . . jerk Glanville was the coach here. It's extra special beating him. When you're stupid, it doesn't bother me, but when you're ignorant, it makes me mad. What the hell has Jerry Glanville ever done in this league?"

Glanville, done up in his black jeans, enormous silver belt buckle, mirrored sun glasses, black boots, and black jacket, strutted onto the field to boos and heard them throughout the game. The man who had said "Texas can kiss my butt" spent most of the fourth quarter listening to a chant of "Jer-ry, Jer-ry, Jer-ry . . ." Then the man who had hugged him and cried when they parted took his shot.

"It's nice to beat Jerry," Bud said. "Any time you can beat Glanville, it's good, because he's the type of guy you like to beat."

Jeff Alm killed himself in 1993. Who knows what an event like that will do to a team? Who knows to this day what it did to the Oilers? The record shows that in their next game they beat the Steelers, 26-17, in Pittsburgh, then won their final two games of the regular season. In this instance, Pardee's temperament was ideal for the situation. As young men wondered what they felt and how they should react, Jack was the same old Jack. They took their cue from him, and moved on.

A strapping specimen out of Notre Dame, Alm had undergone a frightening personality transformation in his four years with the Oilers. The most affable of youngsters when he arrived, he had turned into a snarling brute who picked fights with teammates repeatedly on the practice field and threatened others who crossed his path. A well-regarded second-round draft choice, he had not developed according to expectations and had never risen above part-time starter status. In '93, a seven-game holdout in a contract dispute, a broken leg, and the rapid development of Glenn Montgomery, who was drafted a year before him, limited his playing time at defensive tackle.

Still recovering from his injury, Alm went out on the night of December 13 with his best friend from boyhood days in the Chicago area, Sean Lynch, who was visiting. At a restaurant, they told an employee they planned to attend a party later that evening. Early on Tuesday morning, Alm's '93 Cadillac Eldorado twice struck the guard rail on an elevated freeway ramp on the passenger side. Lynch, who was not wearing a seat belt, was thrown through the open window on the passenger side, hurtling more than 100 feet before dropping 25 feet to his death.

Reconstructing the events from evidence at the scene, police said Alm halted his car, got out, and walked along the railing to peer over at the body of his friend, then walked back to his car and removed a .12-gauge Winchester shotgun with a pistol grip, the same weapon he had pulled on a motorist in a traffic altercation earlier in the year. Spent shells on the ground indicated he fired into the air before putting the barrel into his mouth and pulling the trigger.

Alm had convicted himself of his friend's death. Both men were legally drunk at the time. Alm had been due to return to practice that week in preparation for the Pittsburgh game. Rumors that he had been using anabolic steroids, and some uglier stories, circulated for months after the tragedy.

The Christmas Day victory over the 49ers left only the New York Jets between the Oilers and an 11-game streak and a 12-4 season. The Jets were dispatched with predictable ease, 24-0, but Buddy Ryan would not allow a national television audience to become bored.

Winning streaks and suicides can make a locker room an exceedingly dull place, too placid for Ryan's taste. The Oilers played an oustanding game, but hardly anyone remembered after the defensive coordinator punched the offensive coordinator on the sideline, right there on the tube in front of Paul Tagliabue and everyone.

Shortly before halftime, Ryan flew into a lovely snit when Gilbride made a call in the Houston end of the field that Ryan felt put his defense in a vulnerable position. No harm came of it on the field, but as the teams departed for the lecture halls at the half, Ryan launched a roundhouse right that caught Gilbride a glancing blow. Gilbride, 25 years younger and much closer to fighting trim than his pudgy attacker, started back at Ryan before players intervened.

Even for an owner who had always smirked at the tank as the fighting fish churned the water, this was too much. Adams ordered Holovak and Pardee to meet with the two combatants, and he met with each privately. The owner issued a statement deploring the incident, and Gilbride apologized to the public. Ryan apologized to the players on defense.

To his everlasting credit, Gilbride bottled his bile and put the matter to rest, realizing that any further reaction on his part could tear the team apart just as it entered the playoffs. He also recognized that any additional hostilities would place him in an arena in which Ryan was far more skilled than he. Ryan, of course, wasn't finished.

A day after his meeting with Adams, Ryan did an interview with a Philadelphia reporter he knew well from his days as coach of the Eagles. Saying that Gilbride was running a "high school offense" and "hurting the team," Ryan went on to call his colleague a "wimp" and add that he should be "selling insurance." He said nothing about Gilbride's ancestors or children — in any case, nothing that turned up in print.

The man from Philadelphia had flown in, interviewed Ryan at practice, gone with him to the taping of his weekly television show, and joined him at dinner. Ryan had an explanation: "That's a writer I've known for years. He came here, spent the day with me. That was just the two of us talking. I didn't know it was going to end up in the paper."

A sneak attack, if you will, but perhaps not as sneaky as Ryan had sprung on Gilbride on the sideline.

The Oilers by this time were preparing for their playoff game with the Kansas City Chiefs. After finally winning their division outright, they had dodged the wild-card round and had two weeks to make ready. They were two victories away from their first Super Bowl.

Houston had caught variations on this act so many times before that the city should have been braced, but a fan without hope is no fan at all, and despite what Bud would tell his buds in the owners meetings three years later, Houston had no shortage of fans.

Before a packed house of 64,011, the Chiefs overcame a 10-0 Houston lead and rubbed out the Oilers with 21 fourth-quarter points to win, 28-20, in the Astrodome. Joe Montana, who had repeatedly missed big plays by a whisker in the first half, chopped up Ryan's defense with the heartless efficiency of Big Blue in the second, throwing for three scores. Marcus Allen ran for another and the Oilers limped away in the certain knowledge that they'd never have to say Frank Reich did them in this time.

Just as Rankin Smith had needed a stunt to pull in fans when he hired Jerry Glanville in Atlanta, Bill Bidwill was looking for a freak show to put fannies in seats in Phoenix. He hired Buddy Ryan as head coach and, as in the Atlanta case, the move paid off — for a while.

Bud brought Pardee back for the final year of his contract in 1994, but no one believed, least of all the players. At 1-9, Adams fired Pardee and most of his staff. The season was lost and the Oilers were three weeks away from a date with Ryan's Arizona Cardinals in the Astrodome.

"To this day," said Gilbride, who was heaved out in the purge, after he became head coach of the San Diego Chargers in 1997, "I've never understood why he did that."

12

"Build It, and They Will Come"

Bud Adams himself, true to form, delivered the most damning testimony on the dangers of shuffling teams around a Monopoly board with no regard to tradition.

After an all-time record low crowd of 20,082 turned out to watch his lame-duck team win a 1996 game in the Astrodome with the Baltimore Ravens, he said, "I didn't expect for attendance to be this low, but I'm not that surprised. If the Cleveland Browns had been playing here, I think it would have been a different story because no one knows who the Baltimore Ravens are." The Browns had moved to Baltimore that year and metamorphosed into the Ravens because owner Art Modell couldn't get the new stadium he wanted in Cleveland.

Somehow, no one wrapped his hands around Adams's and began screaming, "Don't you get it yet?"

As for Paul Tagliabue, he has found his long legs an asset in his job as commissioner of the NFL. He has no difficulty at all keeping his feet planted firmly on opposite sides of a fence.

On May 6, 1996, Tagliabue addressed the Downtown Rotary Club in Nashville. After his talk, he told reporters, regarding the Oilers' relocation, "I think this is going to be the last move for a while, yes." As giddy as the city was over gaining a pro football franchise, some could spot a disturbing trend. Los Angeles, Cleveland, and, now, Houston, three of the nation's 10 largest cities, would be without teams. In each case, a team had left a larger television market for a smaller one. "Over time," Tagliabue conceded, "that would be a concern."

On March 8, 1997, at league meetings in Palm Desert, California, the commissioner used Houston as an example of what other naughty league cities might expect if they don't play ball with owners who want new stadiums. He was addressing the situation in Denver, where Broncos owner Pat Bowlen was campaigning for the city to extend a sales tax increase to finance a $180 million investment of public money in a new structure he wanted despite two decades of sellouts at Mile High Stadium.

"The Oilers are a good example of the problem," Tagliabue said. "The Oilers were a very successful football team. Over the course of a decade, they got into the playoffs more than anyone in the league other than perhaps the 49ers, but there was no prospect of a viable stadium in the future and they had to make a decision to protect that future. Hopefully, Denver will make a different decision."

Houston's error, he continued in the gravest of tones, was allowing Bud Adams's personality to become an issue in deliberations over investing at least $150 million of tax money, plus interest, in a new stadium for the enrichment of Bud Adams. If voters in Denver — an election was scheduled for November — should fall into the same abyss of lunacy, the Broncos could be gone.

"That's the most tragic mistake," Tagliabue said. "In Houston, it became a Bud Adams issue. The team is going to be in Nashville in a great new stadium long after Bud Adams is gone unless he has unusual longevity. You don't make your stadium decision based on the popularity of an owner. The issue now is not Pat Bowlen. It's the viability of the franchise, whoever owns it, for the next 40 years. You have to divorce that and sometimes it's hard to do, but it has to be done."

The NFL and its commissioner have no problem in demanding that taxpayers make hard choices, just as they have no difficulty in giving their blessing to the departure of a team from a community that has filled the stands for years. The league rule prohibiting a club in those circumstances from leaving must have come out of a joke book.

The league and its owners are caught between two counterweighing pressures. On the one hand, they wish to project an image of stability and loyalty to the customers. It's difficult to sell the fiction that a franchise has deep roots in a community and that citizens have an emotional investment in it if teams are scattering pell mell across the country to grab sweeter deals. On the other, each owner wants to maximize his revenues. In each case of a conflict, it has been resolved in favor of more loot.

In the league meeting at which the Oilers' move was approved, several owners — including Bowlen — said their misgivings about voting in favor were dissolved by Adams's compelling argument, including his explanation of the dire circumstances he faced in Houston. Next up on their agenda, no doubt, was a presentation on capital punishment by a death-row inmate or the upward pressure on world oil prices by a sheik. Their votes on franchise transfers are merely charades, Al Davis having proved years ago that approval isn't required or legally enforceable, but they continue the practice out of a love for ceremony or simply for amusement. A man can only play so much golf.

Lest we become as cynical as most of them, it's worth noting that a small minority might have sincere concern for faithful fans and for the long-term well-being of their league. Under NFL rules, a franchise transfer must be approved on a three-quarters majority vote, and that's exactly what Adams received. Voting against were Ralph Wilson of Buffalo, Dan Rooney of Pittsburgh, Wellington Mara of the New York Giants, Mike Brown of Cincinnati, Jack Kent Cooke of Washington, and Roger Headrick of Minnesota. Al Davis of Oakland abstained.

Wilson was a co-founding owner of the AFL with Adams. Rooney and Brown control two of the clubs in the Oilers' American Conference Central Division. The owner of the other, Art Modell, was hardly in a position to oppose a move. Tagliabue was Bud's boy all the way. When Pete Rozelle vacated the commissioner's office, Adams had supported Tagliabue in his campaign against Jim Finks, then the president of the New Orleans Saints. After Tagliabue won the job, Adams landed on the powerful finance committee as chairman.

Doris Sherman owns the Orlando Breakers of the NFL on the television sitcom "Coach." When the coach, Hayden Fox, asks her why she wants to move the team from a city where it's making money, she says she can make more money in Los Angeles.

"How much money do you need?" asks Fox.

"How much money is there?" Sherman fires back.

The show is put forth as fiction.

In the real-life NFL, only one club is publicly owned, and thus only one opens its books to the public. The Green Bay Packers play most of their home games in an antiquated stadium, Lambeau Field, that lacks the revenue-producing bells and whistles of the modern palaces. They spent enough money on talent to win the 1997 Super Bowl. And they showed a record profit of $5.9 million for fiscal 1997, up a half-million from the year before. Yet when any NFL owner who seeks a new stadium gives his reason, he says he must generate more revenues so he can buy more talent and keep his team competitive.

Certainly, player payroll costs have risen dramatically since free agency came to the league in 1993. What's more, the salary cap hasn't provided the hard ceiling it was designed to produce because owners have circumvented it by paying huge signing bonuses that are pro-rated over the term of the contract for cap purposes. To afford the fat bonuses, owners say, they must develop new streams of income. That means a state-of-the-art playpen that can throw off from $20 million to — according to some estimates — $40 million in increased annual revenues.

NFL teams cut up network television revenues into equal pieces and split the take on ordinary seats on a 60-40 basis between home and visiting clubs. Each owner keeps the take from luxury suites, club seats, naming rights, and in-house advertising, assuming he has cut a favorable deal with the stadium authority. All the new stadium deals are weighted heavily in favor of the owner, who typically gets the cash generated by the building while tax dollars go to retiring the bonds.

Taxpayers who don't genuflect before the altar of professional sports should consider converting immediately because they pay for the goose bumps whether they're fans or not.

In fact, Houston taxpayers are picking up part of the tab for the new home of Bud Adams's team in Tennessee. Because such projects are financed with municipal bonds, the interest on which the holder

is not required to pay federal income tax, every taxpayer in the country picks up the slack for the tax dollars Washington doesn't receive.
The Congressional Research Service found that a $225 million stadi-
um financed entirely with tax-exempt bonds would get a 30-year subsidy of as much as $75 million.

Some communities, Houston included, that have voted down
bond issues for schools have approved public money for stadiums, and
the full cost isn't always apparent to taxpayers. In most cases, money
that isn't included in the stadium financing package goes to building
roads, freeway access ramps, and other infrastructure requirements.
Whether they're lining their own pockets or those of their millionaire
hired hands — or, most likely, both — megamillionaire owners are
solving their cash-crunch problems — if indeed they do exist — on
the backs of taxpayers, most of whom can't afford a ticket to a game.
And that's not even including the seat license.

The owners' pleas for more cash to attract more stars to keep
"your" team competitive is disingenuous on another level. Even if
they plowed every additional dime from enhanced stadium revenues
into the team, they would make out like counterfeiters on the appreciation in the value of the franchise. And even as the value of the team
jumps at kickoff on the day of the first game in the new stadium, at
that same moment the taxpayers' investment in the facility begins to
depreciate.

America's white-collar criminals owe it to themselves to re-exam-
ine their lives. Why buck the law when deals like this are legal?

We the public can bray at the owners and rail at the players, but we
have inflicted this situation on ourselves. Sports are that important to
us. When Senator Daniel Patrick Moynihan of New York introduced

a bill that would require that sports facilities be financed with bonds that are not tax-exempt, he was hooted down by a chorus composed mainly of self-interested organizations but which included the League of Cities. Lifting the exemption would have made it more difficult to raise capital to build stadiums for rich owners. Cities demanded the right to continue to be raped.

In Houston, the county considered litigation to force Adams to keep his team in town or to pay part of the $67 million spent on the Astrodome when he threatened to take his franchise to Jacksonville. U.S. District Judge Lynn Hughes told lawyers for the county they didn't stand a chance. "There's nothing mystical about a sports franchise," he said. "I don't care if it is a hairdressing salon, an auto repair shop, a professional sports franchise. You have no mystical power over them."

He was undoubtedly right. The fact is that these teams hold all the power, mystical and otherwise, over us. If not, why do we ignore such pressing needs as better schools and improved police protection to throw tax dollars at them? It is not, in most cases, to stimulate economic development. While that argument has been put forth by gung-ho municipal and state officials and, of course, by owners and leagues, the consensus among independent economists is that any economic benefit a community derives is wildly disproportionate to the cost. Some of them have compared the impact to that provided by a Macy's or a Wal-Mart store.

A study commissioned by Mayor Lanier showed that the economic benefit of all three of Houston's big-league franchises, plus other events held in the Astrodome, accounted for less than one percent of the regional economy, or a bit less than that generated by the city's Medical Center. Most economists, however, do concede an intangible gain related to image.

For a Nashville, which has never had big-league sports, the value is greater than to a Houston, which 35 years before — when it was about the size of Nashville — voted tax dollars to build the Astrodome. So frenzied has been the stampede to throw up stadiums to attract teams that the very momentum is now used as an argument in favor: If these franchises aren't attractive and valuable, why are so many cities so hot to get them? The answer might be found in the Greater Fool Theory, but on that score only time will tell.

According to projections, more than $9 billion will be spent around the country on sports venues in the 1990s, and of that staggering sum more than 80 percent will be public money. Citizens in revolt against taxes on virtually every other front will climb into their togas and tick off a "yes" vote for a new Colosseum faster than a lion can munch a Christian. Political conservatives who oppose public funds for private enterprise on principle often can see their way clear to an exception in the case of a stadium. Minority citizens, many of whom won't be able to afford a ticket, often vote in favor as a bloc on the grounds that jobs will be created for their community.

People from all walks of life, it appears, can find a justification for a vote in favor because what they really want is the rush of rooting for "their" team in a Super Bowl or other big-time championship game. Their team is only theirs, of course, as long as they are willing to subsidize players' salaries and owners' profits with tax dollars. If they are not, it will soon "belong" to strangers in another city.

We have handed the NFL and other leagues more leverage than Tiger Woods generates with a driver in his hands; we probably shouldn't be surprised when they use it. Senator Byron Dorgan of North Dakota calls the tax-supported stadium-building craze the "largest public-housing project in America." Houston Mayor Lanier applies the word "shameful" and says, "The subsidy they get is totally disproportionate to the economic benefit they bring. It would shame Jay Gould and his fellow robber barons of the 19th Century. Even Genghis Khan got sated after a while."

Still, after the Oilers' departure became an inevitability, Lanier threw his full support behind a new downtown baseball park heavily dependent on tax dollars after Astros owner Drayton McLane, Jr., threatened to sell his team to interests that would move it.

The differences were dramatic. For one, a ballpark to be used for 81 dates a year could be deployed as the centerpiece in a downtown revitalization effort, as had been done in other cities, whereas a football-only facility would open on 10 days annually. For another, McLane had cultivated the business community, which was called upon for a significant contribution to the project. He could muster allies, whereas Adams had remained aloof and had alienated the same crowd — who, by the way, had bought the luxury boxes in the now-decrepit Astrodome that he had demanded in the late '80s. For a third, McLane had suffered operating losses in the tens of millions since buying the Astros shortly before the players' strike of 1994 whereas Adams had realized a fortune on his $25,000 investment in pro football in 1960.

Still, the mayor turned thumbs down on one tax-funded stadium and up on another. Voters passed the new ballpark in a referendum with 51 percent approving. Lanier also backed a plan for a new basketball/hockey arena, and the voters' O.K. was expected at referendum. Houston wasn't opting out of the franchise free agency hysteria entirely.

To keep the game going, a cartel such as the NFL must ensure that demand for franchises outstrips supply. If every city that wanted one had one, owners would find themselves without leverage. The league thus holds out a carrot to panting cities by telling them they're in regions targeted for expansion while holding the supply of new franchises to a trickle.

After moving his team from Cleveland to Baltimore, Art Modell boasted that he had won new stadiums for five other franchises. He certainly provided that service for at least one. The conservative citizens of Cincinnati were none too keen on tax dollars for new stadiums, but Modell's move lit their fire, and when the smoke cleared they had voted more than $500 million for new venues for both the NFL Bengals and the baseball Reds. Once again, the matter turned on image. The Queen City had been losing industry and feared being relegated to the status of a — gasp — Louisville.

Royalty mustn't be washed downriver and into the backwater of the poor relations.

The NFL's financial athletes weren't the only ones in the game. In addition to the New Jersey Devils, the Florida Panthers of the NHL and the Minnesota Timberwolves of the NBA used Nashville's sparkling and vacant new basketball/hockey arena to get better deals at home. The Houston Astros flirted with a group in Northern Virginia. Rockets owner Leslie Alexander went to court in 1996 in a bid to squirm out of a lease binding his team to The Summit until the end of 2003.

If successful, he would have enjoyed the leverage of a threat to take the city's favorite team elsewhere. He lost, and began campaigning for a split in his favor of revenues from a new arena his club would share with a proposed NHL franchise. Just as former baseball commissioner Fay Vincent had come to town to pitch for a better Astrodome deal for John J. McMullen when he owned the Astros and Tagliabue had carried the ball for Bud, NBA commissioner David Stern showed up during the 1997 playoffs to set a pick for Alexander.

"The most important thing is for a team to get the value it

deserves," said Stern. "I've always thought that when two sides are negotiating, a fair deal is not necessarily 50-50. If you have a team worth $80 million and you have a team worth twice as much as that, there has to be a recognition that the Rockets have a lifetime investment in the city. You can't just say, 'Why don't the Rockets give up their birthright?'"

Whatever that meant.

Baseball's building boom saw five new parks come on line in a five-year span beginning in 1989, all built in large measure with tax dollars. All but one, New Comiskey in Chicago, lived up to their billing. In Baltimore, Cleveland, and Denver, the retro parks — designed to evoke the nostalgia of a bygone day in baseball — became vital pieces in schemes to redevelop decaying downtown districts.

In those cases and in Arlington, Texas, the new facilities generated vastly increased revenues through better attendance, higher ticket prices, more premium seats, restaurants, sports bars, and even shopping malls. The teams' expenditures on talent shot up and club performance improved. Even in cities where schools are falling down, you can't beat tax-subsidized fun at the old ballpark.

Football stadiums do not typically have the same beneficial effect on blighted downtowns although some, as in St. Louis, have been partly justified as adjuncts to convention facilities. The real reason for building them is that citizens are captivated by games and the people who play them. No amount of obscenity, promiscuity, drug abuse, or callous disregard for the team concept or for teammates sours fans across the country, who welcome players back from drug suspension with standing ovations. Youngsters have killed for sneakers endorsed by star athletes. Dennis Rodman flaunts every convention his society embraces, produces a vile and vulgar book replete with references to his sexual activities, and fans in Chicago stand in line for eight hours to have it autographed.

The aura athletes' celebrity generates bathes those associated with them who haven't broken a sweat in years. Both boxing promoter Don King and New York Yankees owner George Steinbrenner were convicted of felonies — although King was later pardoned after serving prison time — and both have appeared in TV commercials. Certain members of the Dallas Cowboys appear intent on assembling rap sheets as long as their lists of Pro Bowl appearances, and yet this remains America's Team. As important to us as sports and athletes obviously are, perhaps it should come as no surprise that we're willing to pay several times to have them among us.

In football, new stadium technology has made big-league players of minor-league towns. If a prosperous small city such as Nashville can scrape together $292 million, plus interest — in many cases, as this one, with the help of the state — it can put up a stadium that promises in theory to produce enough revenue to turn an owner's head. If it guarantees that income, as Nashville did, *voilà*. The city goes on the hook and the owner goes on a cruise.

This is the new capitalism in sports. In the football realm, it's too early in the game to determine whether or not the intangible benefit of a spiffier image justifies the expenditure of public money. Experts in corporate relocation say companies do often examine the sports culture along with other amenities in a city they're considering. They also say such concerns rank well down the list, after health care, safe streets, affordable housing, and, yes, good schools.

Tax dollars support museums, parks, zoos, symphonies, ballets, and operas, all without question assets to a community. Chimpanzees and cellists come less dear than Chargers and Chiefs, however, and they do not threaten to hit the road if their quarters don't measure up to those in Cleveland.

So voracious have sports owners become that they now demand single-purpose facilities in football and baseball. These stadiums can be configured to accomodate the greatest possible numbers of seats with optimum sightlines, seats that can be sold at a premium, as well as strategically positioned luxury boxes. If each owner controls a stadium, too, no owner must pay rent to or share revenues with another. In Nashville, Adams will play landlord to other events in the stadium. Luxury box owners, incidentally, will enjoy the use of their suites for non-football events — but they'll be required to buy a ticket.

If NFL owners are indeed victims of a salary spiral brought on by free agency, they're also using public money to buy absolution from sins of their own. In some markets, ticket sales have softened, in no small measure because the club did absolutely nothing in the way of marketing. Davis cut the heartstrings of the adoring masses in Oakland when he hauled his Raiders down the coast to Los Angeles, then assumed his team would find the same rabid following upon its return. In anticipation of such, he instituted a league-high average ticket price of $51 and quickly found his swashbucklers playing to crowds smaller than those they had left in laid-back El Ay.

Other sports jumped into the fray. Some might be classified as junk sports, but they staked out a share of the entertainment dollar. NFL teams accustomed to marking lines on the field (and hoping the players didn't snort them up), throwing open the gates, and listening to the sweet cha-ching of the cash register discovered they needed to market and didn't know how. Some clubs under stress at the gate couldn't seem to get beyond dancing girls as they groped for sideshows to gussy up the entertainment experience even though the NBA had long before established the blueprint.

At Utah Jazz playoff games at the Delta Center in Salt Lake City, balloons spill down from the rafters and fireworks shower fans in expensive courtside seats with smoking debris to suggest the last days of Pompeii. That's in addition to the mascot in the bear suit who somersaults through burning hoops to a slam dunk and dancers gyrating to suggestive lyrics that would send Brigham Young back into the desert in search of a place to start anew.

For those who will only open their eyes, there are ways to put pizzazz in a boring old ballgame.

While television and luxury-suite revenues have rendered gate receipts less important than they once were, NFL executives know they'll never get away with producing a studio show. Throaty fans attached to the fannies that are attached to the seats are necessary to create a spectacle that plays on TV. Still, some franchises were slow to bring in marketing experts and even to accept help from a division of the league office set up to assist in pushing tickets.

Back at the frat house, the horseplay got a bit rough, too. Members of the cartel had always been team players, but free agency for the athletes provided a justification for abusing one another along with taxpayers. After a couple of other owners did modest deals for stadium advertising, Dallas maverick Jerry Jones went wild with contracts with Nike, American Express, and Pepsi that put league sponsorship agreements in jeopardy. Lawsuits flew.

Not every owner could get a new stadium, at least not as soon as he wanted one, and talk circulated of changing the rules so that the nouveau riche would be forced to share more of their new wealth with the less fortunate. For Adams, for example, if stadium revenues in Nashville hit a modestly estimated $20 million annually, he will have quintupled that income stream. Enough of the emirs got their new palaces quickly enough, however, that those left out couldn't muster the three-fourths majority necessary to amend the rules. Baseball-style turf wars had come to the once-chummy NFL, but the situation was far from grim.

Back in the 1960s, the AFL had become a player capable of forcing a merger with the established league because a television network had rolled the dice on additional sports programming. Thirty years later, nothing much had changed except the zeroes. In the same way that golf before Tiger Woods commanded higher advertising rates than bare ratings numbers could justify because of an audience that could afford to drive Cadillacs and Great Big Berthas, football ruled the demographics. The only difference was the exponent. The game delivers young men with cash in their pockets by the millions, and networks pay such a premium to get them — in the hope they can keep them with other shows — that they take a loss on football.

The NFL's slick kids on Park Avenue see all of television as one never-ending episode of "Wheel of Fortune," and they're good at the game. Just as they keep demand high in the franchise free agency arena, they make sure there's always at least one network that wants their game that doesn't get it. With cities fighting to provide gold mines for owners in the form of new stadiums and networks battling for the right to continue deficit-spending on football, the NFL has been riding high. Owners griped about soaring player costs, but Dr. No, Pussy Galore, and Jaws combined couldn't pry a franchise away from one of them.

In 1997, Houston joined Los Angeles and Cleveland on the outside looking in. The league had given up Los Angeles, the nation's second-largest market, for No. 20 St. Louis and part of No. 5 San Francisco-Oakland, and No. 13 Cleveland for No. 23 Baltimore.

Now it was swapping No. 11 Houston for No. 33 Nashville. Dick Ebersol, the NBC sports chief, said he was "troubled" by the trend. NFL television ratings declined across the board. But as the summer of 1997 began to shimmer, networks were arming themselves for a struggle for rights that industry analysts figured to raise the league's $1.1 billion-a-year TV revenues by as much as 40 percent.

With the explosion of cable channels cutting into the prime-time ratings on all of the traditional Big Three networks, each viewed the NFL as a vehicle for promoting prime-time shows. On ABC, "Monday Night Football" was the highest-rated show. NBC saw in pro football as well a strong lead-in for Sunday night programming, and CBS, which had given way to Fox in the last go-round, wanted back in for the same reasons. Since it lost football, "60 Minutes" had fallen out of the top 10.

Fox, which had ponied up $395 million a year, took a $350 million write-off against its losses on NFL telecasts in 1995 and didn't blink. The Super Bowl provided the highest rating in the company's history and probably the top-rated show of the year on any network. Fox's prime-time ratings had risen seven percent since the NFL came on board. Beavis and Butthead owed a lot to Paul Tagliabue.

Just as Bud Adams had parlayed a team that never won into a property Tennessee considered a bargain at any price, the NFL was set to cash in slipping television ratings, losses in the tens of millions for the networks, and attrition of major markets for another windfall from television. Paul Tagliabue owed a lot to Beavis and Butthead.

Houston is no Cleveland, never even had a Dawg Pound. When Cleveland voters levied a sin tax on themselves and erected glitzy facilities for the city's baseball and basketball teams, Browns owner Art

Modell couldn't take it any more. His Browns had performed at a much higher level in the arena than the Indians and Cavaliers, but they remained in dilapidated Municipal Stadium — the Mistake by the Lake — while the owners of the other franchises bathed luxuriously in the revenue streams generated by new buildings.

As in Houston, local leaders had been caught in a priorities crunch. The Indians were losing money and couldn't survive forever — or, likely, much longer — in Municipal Stadium. The Cavaliers had defected to the suburb of Richfield and could only be wooed back with a new building. The Browns could wait. When Cuyahoga County officials found it a struggle to service the debt on the new pleasure palaces with the dollars produced by the sin tax, they could hardly justify added expenditures for a football stadium.

Modell's reaction: "They lied to me."

He saw the cash-burping new edifices of the Indians and Cavaliers and took a look around at the new stadiums either operating or on the drawing boards in the NFL, and he wanted one, too. Baltimore, which lost out in the most recent expansion round, had left an open invitation on the table. The city had been without a team since Robert Irsay packed up the Colts and rolled them down the highway in unmarked moving vans in the dead of night in 1984. (In 1997, by the way, the Colts were demanding a tax-funded renovation of the RCA Dome in Indianapolis to include more premium seats and a break on the rent.)

Like St. Louis and Oakland, Baltimore wanted pro football back regardless of the abuse or cost involved. Modell jumped at the offer of a $200 million stadium. When he struck the deal, the value of his franchise shot up to an estimated $160 million, or 25 percent.

Leaving Cleveland in the lurch, however, proved trickier for the NFL than waving ta-ta. The city mobilized as though the enemy were beaching on the Lake Erie shore. Fans jammed fax machines at league offices and those of its clubs. Rabies raged through the Dawg Pound. The rowdies known across the nation for painting their faces, strapping on snouts, and throwing dog biscuits, snow balls, and less forgiving objects at opposing players from their end-zone seats trekked to Washington in game-day splendor and barked at Congress.

Representative Martin Hoke of Ohio introduced legislation that would require the NFL to give a city that lost a franchise a replacement. While never given a serious chance of passing, it put the league-wide building boom on hold. In Nashville, the delay pushed back the completion date for the Bud Hole by a year. The NFL peered into this maelstrom and its knees wobbled. The league promised Cleveland another team within four years, contingent on a new stadium, and allowed the city to keep the Browns' name. Cleveland decided it could take on more sports-related debt, after all, and began planning a football facility that would push its investment in structures for sports past $600 million.

In Houston, a "Save the Oilers" rally at City Hall attracted an impassioned crowd of 50.

American cities vary widely in their attitudes toward sports, and the split occurs almost exactly along the Mason-Dixon Line. Several factors come into play, among them the longevity of a team in its community and the number of generations that have invested their hopes and fears in it, the stability of an area's population, and the pace of life. No other, however, is as important as weather.

Houston's sub-tropical climate allows access to year-round outdoor activities eliminated or seriously curtailed for several months each year in the Northeast and Midwest. Golf, tennis, fishing — both saltwater and freshwater — hunting, and boating are all within an easy drive. All compete with spectator sports for money and for time.

Teams draw well when they win, suffer at the gate when they don't. Absent winning on a grand scale, pro football will never pack the stands in Houston as the Redskins, Giants, and Bears do, and you can book it.

In that way, Houston is typical of the Sun Belt. The expansion Florida Marlins opened to a massive yawn in Miami. Before they began making annual visits to the World Series, the Atlanta Braves played to crowds of 3,000, and the Hawks, still searching for the secret, couldn't fill the Omni with cash rebates on tickets. The San Diego Padres struggled at the gate until a new owner arrived with a cash infusion that resulted in a division championship. In the 1995-96 season, before Magic Johnson made his late-season comeback, the Los Angeles Lakers ranked 25th in the NBA in attendance despite a glorious tradition.

The NFL isn't exempt. In Atlanta, New Orleans, Phoenix, San Diego, and Los Angeles, crowds have slumped along with the teams. Even America's Team played to patches of empty seats in Texas Stadium during the down years of Tom Landry's dotage and Jimmy Johnson's inaugural.

Where the sun shines, people can find better entertainment than bad football.

And then there's Bud. Tagliabue was right when he said Houston allowed the owner's personality to color its thinking on a new football stadium. As polls showed, an overwhelming majority rejected spending public money for a new stadium for his team while sentiment split evenly on tax dollars for a building for another owner. The mayor supported and voters approved, if by a slim margin, public funds for a downtown baseball park. Adams maintained that decision came in response to the Oilers' departure, that the verdicts would have been reversed if the Astros had first cut a deal to flee. His was perhaps a generous assessment.

After the fact of the move had settled in, Bud's Adams Resources & Energy, Inc., went to trial against a plumbing contractor in a dispute over a leak that had caused a flood in the Oilers' basement offices and fouled the phone system. Adams wanted $25,000 in damages. When the defendant's lawyer asked during jury selection if anyone would find it difficult to give Adams a fair trial, hands shot up as at a meeting of the Waffen SS.

"We managed to seat a jury," said the counselor, "but only after the judge indicated that they should not decide the merits of the case on their like or dislike of Mr. Adams." In the end, incidentally, those feelings were not an issue. Bud's team fumbled some key points — for one, its "expert" witness was not a licensed plumber — and the judge threw the case out of court.

How prospective jurors might have responded five years earlier we'll never know, but Bud was never Houston's pin-up boy. He fired Bum Phillips, haggled endlessly over contracts with draft choices who often showed up for training camp too late to do the team much good, allowed the team's front-office staff to go years without raises, operated a practice facility that was finally replaced long after it had become an embarrassment, and allowed Ladd Herzeg and Jerry Glanville to heap indignities on the franchise and the city.

He extorted a $67 million Astrodome redo with a threat to leave town and, long before his lease was up, began screaming for more tax dollars for an entirely new building. Save for one modest annual fund-raiser, he remained aloof from charities and kept the business community at a distance. He demanded a domed football/basketball facility and, when the Rockets owner said he'd pass, refused to discuss other options, instead signing an exclusive negotiating agreement with Nashville.

You're damned right, Mr. Commissioner. Houston let it get personal.

Besides, Bud knew how to get personal as well. Soon after he began his dalliance with Jacksonville, Houston mayor Kathy Whitmire figured she should act. Although the football facility was county-owned, she reasoned that if the team left on her watch, the mayor would get the blame. Whitmire, often called "Mayor Tootsie" for her striking resemblance to the Dustin Hoffman character in the movie *Tootsie*, arranged a meeting with Adams.

She arrived at his basement office — "the Bunker" — with aide Paul Mabry and City Councilman Jim Greenwood. They sat in a conversation pit with the owner, Ladd Herzeg, and Tommy Smith, Bud's son-in-law and a team executive. After the exchange of pleasantries, Whitmire opened the meeting's business by asking Adams, "What can we do to keep the Oilers in Houston?"

Herzeg and Smith knew what was coming. Smith buried his head in his hands and said, "I'm not responsible for this." Herzeg, according to one who was there, "started bouncing on the couch like a little kid."

And Bud said, "Mayor, I've got a little office in back with a fold-out couch if you'd like to discuss it further."

So Bud never minded making things personal.

13

Rosin Up
Them Bows

The question did arise. In an appearance before Nashville's Metro Council, Bud Adams fielded it with his usual light-footed grace. Why Nashville?

"Baltimore's not my cup of tea," Bud bantered. "And Los Angeles, that's the home of the nuts and the fruits out there."

Reassured, Nashville pressed on.

One of the city's former mayors had played the harmonica — and the fool — on "The Phil Donahue Show." Phil Bredesen would not make that mistake. A Harvard graduate with a degree in physics, he rolled up a net worth in excess of $100 million as founder and CEO of Health/America Corporation. If his talents carried him into business, however, his instincts constantly tugged him toward politics.

Bredesen, who grew up in upstate New York, lost a bid for a seat in the Massachusetts state senate in the early 1970s. After his career in health care took him to Nashville — the city is such a strong regional center for the industry that the city-limits signs could read, "A great place to get sick" — he lost in the 1987 mayoral race and then a bid for a seat in the U.S. House of Representatives. He won election as mayor in 1991, failed in a '94 crack at the Tennessee governor's mansion and secured re-election as mayor in '95.

If one is forced to endure as a local politician, Nashville isn't a bad place to dig in. Its metro government incorporates what in many other municipalities are city, county, and school administrations under one umbrella, and the mayor's office is stronger than corn likker. And that's just the sort of allusion Bredesen was out to snuff.

In interviews with national publications, he said when Americans outside the area conjure images of his adopted hometown they see "hillbillies, hay bales, and gingham dresses." He made no mention of possum on the dinner table.

"As someone who both talks to people around the country and travels around the country," he added, "I can assure you that when the name 'Nashville' is mentioned, it is synonymous with country music, which is synonymous with 'Hee-Haw' . . . That's like saying that New York is about nothing but getting mugged."

In his search for an analogous misconception, he might have chosen better, but we take the point. In one of those mystical confluences of phenomena none can explain, a city and a team came together because Bredesen's passion to do something profoundly good for Nashville's image flamed as brightly as Bud Adams's passion to do something profoundly good for Bud. It was a match made in a fiddler's heaven.

The wily Bredesen might have omitted most of Adams's history when he regaled the citizens with the raptures of having real, live, professional athletes in town, but it probably didn't matter. Nashville was sold. Either the good folks had been to the Grand Ole Opry so many times they were bored stiff or they didn't care if Joseph Goebbels were the owner as long as somebody with a football team arrived to rake the straw from their teeth and cure their image. Many of them even saluted the mayor's plan to dip into their water-and-sewer fund in the effort to finance the $292 million Bud Hole on the east bank of the Cumberland River, this despite water rates already second-highest in the country. In man-on-the-street interviews, they gushed of how their new team would "go all the way" with the strong support of a rabid Tennessee following.

At the bottom line, the reason Adams's team left Texas for Tennessee is that Nashville was far more concerned with perception than was Houston. In both cities, many urban needs generally regarded as more pressing — in lip service, anyway — competed for the tax dollars that would go into a football stadium. In Nashville, Bredesen said, "This football team is very important to us. I realize that it will never directly pay back the cost to taxpayers to build it, but that is one giant amenity." In Houston, Mayor Bob Lanier said, "It's very hard for me to go into neighborhoods that need street lights and sidewalks and police and parks and ask those people for money for a stadium they probably can't afford to buy tickets for." Both leaders reflected the majority views in their communities.

Houston wasn't without image worries. At about the time the Oilers' departure was getting the finishing touches, coincidentally, the mayor named a committee headed by his wife to address that issue. And Nashville, while a much smaller city, had no vaccination against urban blight. Stadium opponents found no shortage of projects they considered more worthwhile.

The city was under a court order to desegregate its schools and the cost of a plan to end busing was pegged at $90 million. Over the previous five years, the violent crime rate had jumped 42 percent. The needy receiving Aid to Families with Dependent Children in Tennessee were limited to $220 a month for 18 months.

Others voiced philosophical objections. "As a legislator," said State Representative Mike Kernell, D-Memphis, "I have a real problem with state money going to a gang of millionaires Houston now hates. This is taxation for the poor and socialism for the rich. It's taxation for women and children and socialism for a bunch of rich millionaires."

Bud might have bristled when the law-maker used the plural. Even the team's ladies auxiliary, the dance squad, took some hits. "There is nothing I aspire to less," said Councilman David Kleinfelter, "than for my daughter to grow up to be a Derrick Doll. It is sexism incarnate."

The proponents' reaction? At the meeting at which Kleinfelter raised his concern, his council colleague Ronnie Steine remarked, "To be honest with you, this was an opportunity for those opposed to this to get a little tube time."

They could afford a cavalier attitude. Even after a property-tax hike financed an arena that squatted downtown without a basketball or hockey tenant at the time the football stadium plan was finalized, Nashville was gung-ho for Bud. Early in the process, Bredesen floated the possibility of another increase in property taxes, which would have been the area's second in three years. So assured were the pro-stadium forces that Councilman Steine disclosed the strategy in public: "The mayor can be a hero when he brings back something else [other than the property tax increase]."

After anti-stadium forces gathered sufficient signatures on a petition to force a referendum, advocates still didn't break a sweat. After an initial projection of $1 million in advertising expenditures, they actually laid out $400,000 (to $25,000 for the opposition). Polling indicated that 62 percent of citizens believed an NFL team would generate a net revenue gain for the area, 67 percent were convinced of a benefit to the local economy and 79 percent agreed with the mayor's contention that the city's image would be festooned. At the polls, 59 percent voted in favor of the $292 million project. And when they looked around, Bud was gone.

The absentee owner flew back to Houston before the polls closed, electing not to address the throng of supporters who waited out the returns in a stifling warehouse and celebrated a deal that would bump his annual revenues by $25 million — a figure that holds even if his team never wins a game, even if after a few years the new wears off and attendance takes a nosedive.

That possibility isn't as remote as Bredesen and his allies might wish. Los Angeles never embraced the Raiders, and Phoenix turned off to the Cardinals faster than you can say, "Bill Bidwill." Based on attendance at the University of Tennessee's 106,000-seat stadium in Knoxville, the state qualifies as a football hotbed. In Austin, however, the University of Texas team draws so well that a law banning new construction that blocks sightlines to the dome of the state capitol has been waived to permit addition of a second deck to the stadium, yet in down years both the Oilers and the Dallas Cowboys have played to empty seats.

Because Greater Nashville comprises a relatively small population base, even officials of that city admit, a statewide effort will be required to support Adams in the style to which he will soon be accustomed, that of Jabba the Hut, another round dude with massive appetites. The good citizens of Memphis, alas, hold their richer relations in the middle of the state in contempt and have even less regard for the NFL. Memphis feels it was betrayed when the league awarded the expansion franchise for which it believed it had a commitment to Jacksonville. Now, Nashville is getting the pros, and all the economic benefits that will allegedly accrue, and the entire state is sharing in the stadium cost.

It bears noting as well that eastern Tennessee harbors an abiding affection for the Washington Redskins and that the Atlanta Falcons, nearer to Chattanooga than to Savannah or Valdosta, enjoy a following in the state as well. Since the NFL's most recent expansion, in fact, Dixie claims almost as many pro football teams as stock-car tracks.

In neighboring North Carolina, the Carolina Panthers play in Charlotte and, unbeknownst to Nashville's negotiators when they were handing the lock to the city to Adams, the Panthers were turning into a snarling outfit in only their second year of existence. Already, they are regarded among the elite teams of the National Conference.

In the years to come, the Adams Family will find spirited competition not only for the entertainment dollar in Tennessee but for command of remote controls as well. As for the NFL's smug contention that cities such as Houston that lose teams sprout couch potatoes on Sunday afternoons like toadstools after a rain, it's a good story to feed to the networks and advertisers, at least those who don't investigate too deeply. In the season after Southern Callifornia lost both the Raiders and the Rams, the league's ratings in the area plummeted by more than 33 percent.

Of course, Bud isn't required to care.

"It's truly wonderful to be wanted by a city and a community," he said by phone of the successful referendum, having flown home to execute an oil lease.

Bredesen said he wasn't alarmed at Adams's early departure: "He was always here when we needed him."

On that tender note, Nashville became a big-league city. Whether it fixed its hayseed image by seducing Bud is another matter, but at least it didn't get Ladd Herzeg in the bargain.

In Houston, Adams told a sympathetic reporter, "When I made the trip to Nashville to sign the papers, they put that last page in front of me and I was still thinking, 'Do I really want to do this? Do I really want to move?' I was holding the fountain pen and my hand was shaking." Somehow, he collected himself and got his name on the line, but it would be foolish to suggest that pulling his team out of the city that had been his home for half a century came without an emotional price.

Veteran Bud-watchers concluded almost unanimously that the little man who never seemed quite sure of his course was caught up in a swift current that deposited him on the east bank of the Cumberland River before he realized he had been washed off the bank of Buffalo Bayou.

Over the years, Adams had been alternately prominent in the operation of his team and almost invisible, committed to spending money to get top players and dedicated to pinching pennies, absolutely certain that he had hired the coach that would take the Oilers to the Super Bowl and just as convinced a year or two later that his successor was that man. Herzeg had found manipulating his boss so easily managed that he had ample time left over for more entertaining and challenging endeavors.

Mike McClure lacked Herzeg's steel-trap mind and the easy charm he could switch on like a starlet's smile before his weakness for bubbles and Bubbles corroded both, but McClure sharpened his cunning on a grindstone from which he never strayed for trivial pursuits. Mike McClure kept his pants up.

14

THE
ART OF
THE DEAL

When McClure returned from his exile in Chicago, he needed a storyline and he needed one quick. Herzeg, telling Joann DeNicola he didn't want to pay her lawyers, had hitched up his britches and hit the road, and McClure had Adams's undivided attention. He chose to trash the deal Herzeg had made with Harris County, which owns the Astrodome, at the time of the Jacksonville scam. As with all good yarns, it wasn't devoid of truth. That arrangement was hardly ideal for either party.

McClure could argue that the NFL's salary cap was rising annually and that more revenues were needed to keep pace. Even a renovated Astrodome was no match for some of the league's more modern palaces. The luxury suites weren't as fancy and didn't fetch as high a price. The stadium, constructed as a multi-purpose facility, offered only 20,000 of its 60,000 seats between the 20-yard lines, the area that commands premium prices. What's more, as a tenant of the baseball owner, Adams derived nothing from other events in the building, and his take on ancillary revenues such as concessions and parking lagged behind those of many of his fellow football moguls. He paid an annual rent of up to $3 million, depending on attendance and revenues.

From the county's perspective, the error came in exacting only a 10-year lease in exchange for the $67 million redo, which did benefit both the Astros and the Houston Livestock Show and Rodeo to a lesser extent. That contract had run scarcely more than half its course, and here was Adams rattling sabers and demanding a grander edifice financed primarily with tax dollars.

When his — or McClure's — threats fell on deaf ears, McClure took a look around and quickly targeted Nashville, which had watched such mid-sized cities as Charlotte and Jacksonville catch NFL franchises and flash their skylines on national television. Bredesen and others wanted a piece of that action. "We've baited a lot of hooks and put out a lot of lines for pro sports," Bredesen said. "It was nice to get a nibble from a great big barracuda."

From the day McClure placed his first call to Tennessee, events proceeded at a pace neither the Oilers nor "Hee-Haw" had ever known. Junior Samples could only have shaken his head. Every time McClure demanded a bag of loot, Nashville said, "Take two; they're small." Governor Don Sundquist balked at chunking in the state's $84.3 million share of financing, but only briefly. Measures approving the expenditures sailed through the legislature and the Metro Council. When the sale of personal seat licenses slowed, threatening a milestone built into the contract, Bredesen prevailed on local banks to guarantee the shortfall.

One morning Adams woke up lying on a feather bed right out of a dream. Appraisers said the new Chez Bud, on the day it opens, will make his franchise, at $220 million, the second most valuable in the league, behind only the Dallas Cowboys.

If Adams at first entertained thoughts of using Nashville as leverage as he had with Jacksonville, his new hosts chased them from his consciousness like wispy white clouds. Spasms of negotiation by capitulation propelled the deal so quickly that Houston couldn't have matched it if the owner's sternest critics had all suddenly married into his family.

For one thing, Governor George W. Bush remained adamantly opposed to spending state funds for stadiums and promised to veto any bill authorizing such. "This is not a state matter," said Bush. "There will be no state money. We are not going to compete with the state of Tennessee for sports franchises." For another, Houston simply had too many big-city problems that demanded cash. For a third, even as anti-Adams sentiment softened as the prospect of losing pro football became more and more real, too many in government, the business community — which had pledged to buy the 66 luxury suites in the renovated Astrodome — and the public would never be able to wash out the sour taste of another raid on the coffers so soon after the previous heist. There's not that much Listerine in the world.

In hard-dollar terms relating only to jobs created, a new stadium in Houston costing $250 million (and assuming it were fully funded with public money) would have generated about 1,000 jobs, meaning a tax subsidy of $250,000 for every job. Local government had spent about $7,500 for every job created when Compaq Computer Corporation had expanded, and the regional average was $4,800 in tax subsidies for each job created.

As the inevitability of watching the moving vans roll out of town along Interstate 10 dawned, some hard-core football fans focused their wrath on the mayor, but their sniping missed the mark. They contended Lanier could have saved the day with inspired leadership if not for his personal animosity toward Adams. In fact, Boss Tweed couldn't have turned this avalanche around.

Their enmity did give the jowly Lanier, ever quicker on the draw than Adams, a chance to exercise his wit. When he voiced his hope that Bud would use his chairmanship of the NFL's finance committee to help in attracting another team to Houston, as Art Modell had promoted Cleveland's cause, Adams said, "I'm not dealing with the mayor. I don't trust the mayor. I wouldn't deal with him as long as he's in office."

Lanier shot back: "That's like being called ugly by a bullfrog."

But there was the matter of the lease. In the settlement of a lawsuit in which he contended the city, county, and Astrodome USA — which owned the Astrodome lease — were interfering with his efforts to negotiate a deal elsewhere, Adams gave each of those entities separately the ability to block his move before his contract in Houston expired following the 1997 season. Adams struck a negotiating posture by maintaining in public that he had no intention of pulling the team out of Houston before his lease expired.

The team's marketing surveys indicated attendance in Houston, even on a lame-duck basis, would outstrip that at Liberty Bowl Memorial Stadium in Memphis, the only viable interim site in Tennessee. Adams said he knew no dread of sending out a team of short-timers in Houston. "These are real football fans," he said. "If we get off to a winning start, I think they'll come. They always have in the past." Those projections flew out the window at the end of the '96 season.

After an auspicious beginning on the field that generated three turnouts in the 50,000 range, the predictable late-season swoon sent the number plummeting to the 20,000 mark for the final two games.

McClure, who had long since taken up residence in Nashville, dickered some more in Memphis, procuring a deal under which Adams would pay a rental of $1 per paid ticket and the stadium authority would pick up about $300,000 annually in travel costs for the team to commute between its Nashville practice facility and its temporary home for games. That money would come from a sales-tax rebate on game-day revenues.

All parties in Houston had grown weary of the process, and Lanier had given up on using the threat of forcing Adams to serve out his lease as leverage with the league to get the promise of a replacement franchise. The city accepted reimbursement of legal fees, the county the deed to the team's practice facility, and Astrodome USA the termination of a lawsuit Adams had filed in which he contended cancelation of an exhibition game had resulted from his landlord's negligence in maintaining the artificial-turf playing field. The county and Astrodome USA also received cash settlements. Buying out of the final year cost Adams $4.1 million, $3.5 million to be paid out to the county over four years. On the Nashville end, he received $28 million in moving expenses.

In June, 1997, the Oilers waltzed out of Houston and off to Tennessee.

And the Oilers they remained. Retaining the name was just one of the surprises Adams, McClure, and their new best friends in Nashville had in store for the electorate.

When he was giving away the still, Bredesen had demanded one and only one major concession from Adams — an assurance that he wouldn't blow town. Why that concern even crossed his honor's mind he didn't say, but he was steadfast in including tough penalties for an early departure. The result was a provision for the franchise to pay $117 million for abandoning Nashville in the first 12 years of the 30-year deal, $87 million in the next 10 years and $34 million in the final eight. Responding to a question in Nashville about his fidelity, Bud said with a straight face:

"I put some high penalties in there, so high that I can't afford to leave."

When he discovered Nashvillians weren't offended by that bit of lyrical wit, Bud gathered steam. "My proudest accomplishment," he said, "is I've kissed the same woman every night for 49 years. I won't say it's a record, but it's quite a while. When Bud Adams tells you he will come if you live up to your end of the bargain, that's binding."

Even Al Davis would have turned red at such rhetoric. As a matter of fact, he did. "It's just crazy to me what's going on with these leases and the lessons we're learning," the man who invented the game of franchise free agency said at an owners meeting.

"People who vote on the rules are the ones breaking them. The one thing you can say about the Raiders is that we never moved until our lease was up. Look at the guys who were on the finance committee. Adams, Modell, and Ken Behring (the Seattle Seahawks owner) are trying to break their leases. They're the ones trying to move. None of these guys meet our guidelines, but they're moving. I don't think Houston meets the guidelines. I still think an owner should have the right to move, but the league should back our guidelines."

At the owners meeting at which the Oilers' move was approved, Davis abstained from voting.

One reason the owners were so accommodating to Adams, Modell, and others was that they assessed a relocation fee each time a club hopped from one city to another. The one exception was the Raiders' return to Oakland. Officially, the reason was that the league hadn't targeted the Bay Area city as an "expansion opportunity." The lodge brothers might also have been scared witless of their renegade sibling, who had already waffled them in court. In the case of the Oilers, the fee was pegged at $25 million.

That eventuality had not been explained to Nashville voters even though the city was responsible for 80 percent of the sum. A $30 million contingency fund had been built into the stadium financing package. After the relocation hit, only $10 million remained to cover cost overruns. Byron Trauger, a local lawyer who served as Bredesen's chief negotiator, produced this artful explanation: "That contingency fund was as large as it was in order to include the relocation fee. It was not spelled out on a separate line item as 'NFL relocation fee' because we didn't want to suggest to the NFL that they impose a relocation fee."

The owners might have forgotten it. They might have forgotten to breathe.

Surprise, surprise. But wait, there's more. Written into the deal was a provision that the club could reduce its annual rent to $362,000 by electing not to require the city to build a practice facility that was part of the package. Less than the lease on a good apartment in New York, that sum was only $111,000 more than Tennessee State University's annual rent, and the school would use the new stadium for far fewer games. The practice facility would have cost the city $9 million. When the club opted to make separate arrangements for a place to sweat, the city lost out on $19 million over 30 years.

Some eager fans took a dose of reality that went down like cod liver oil when they rushed to buy a personal seat license. The PSL, which was not invented by an accountant for the mob, gives the purchaser the right to buy a ticket attached to that seat. In Nashville,

PSLs were sold on five-, seven- and 10-year contracts. Because the stadium pricing structure was top-heavy with club seats, the relatively few more affordable loge seats were snapped up quickly, and sale of the pricier PSLs lagged.

Elizabeth Beatty, a fan who sent in her application as soon as they were offered, said, "I really see this as a bait-and-switch. We applied for a certain price, which they advertised, then they turn around and tell us it's not available and we have to buy a much more expensive seat. It this were done at a furniture store, it would be against the law."

Some were shocked to learn the final cost of the $292 million project would be approximately $500 million, including interest on the massive debt. When that number came to light, advocates said soothingly that it's common knowledge that a borrower pays interest on a loan, as in the purchase of a house. Opponents snapped back that in such a case the lender is required to reveal the amount of interest involved, and voters hadn't been informed.

Nowhere in the contract was there a mandate that the team change its name. On that score, Nashville trusted the word of the man who had kissed the same woman every night for 49 years. It probably seemed so natural a thing that no legal imprimatur was required. That, after all, was how Bud had treated it.

"The Oilers didn't seem to be the right name for Tennessee unless someone knows a place around here where some oil might be coming out of the ground," he told a gathering in the Davidson County courthouse foyer, getting a round of laughs. "This is going to be Tennessee's team."

McClure was more specific. "NFL Properties, the marketing arm of the NFL, is screening several names," he said, "to make sure there are no conflicts with existing teams, businesses, or individuals to avoid conflicts, litigation or control by another entity. After the search, anywhere from eight to 10 or even 15 names will be submitted in a statewide contest. Tennessee fans will make the final decision."

Adams mentioned "Fiddlers" and "Pioneers" as possibilities. After the deal was complete, he said he thought he'd hang on to the old name, citing a sentimental attachment.

The Oilers, as we still know them, took control of marketing the stadium's luxury suites, from which Adams would derive all revenue. Then they refused to divulge the names of buyers, citing a confidentiality agreement. McClure, usually judicious in his public utterances, in this case had to gild the lily. "It also raises a public-safety concern to name the individuals," he explained. "Many of those who have purchased the suites are individuals who will be away from their domiciles for five hours every Sunday."

The safety concern, if any, was quite private, and this gibberish was too much even for the Nashville media, which had chronicled the process from the beginning with less than a jaundiced eye. After the state's attorney general ruled the information was in the public domain because tax dollars were flowing into the stadium, McClure kicked loose the names.

Irby Simpkins, publisher of the *Nashville Banner*, which had sought the information under the state's open-records law, then said, "Mike McClure and the Houston Oilers have settled this matter with a handshake with me. Those are the kinds of business people that Nashvillians need to get to know in this important public-private partnership."

After all the posturing by persons in positions of authority, an ordinary fan probably expressed Nashville's attitude best. A tailgate party outside the courthouse attracted 2,500 citizens. One was Angela Burum, a 36-year-old secretary who stood in line for free hot dogs wearing a T-shirt reading "Tennessee ???" in anticipation of a new name for the team. "I don't care if they raise my water rates or what," she said. "I love the NFL. Whatever it costs, it's worth it."

Over 30 years, it will cost a half-billion dollars. Thirty years earlier, baseball was America's Pastime and the National Basketball Association was on the verge of collapse. Tiger Woods wouldn't be born for another nine years, and golf was still a game of the rich. Auto racing was strictly for guys with grease under their fingernails, and the gals who loved them.

Fashions change, tastes change.

With the blessing of his boss, Mike McClure collected $1 million from Nashville interests for services rendered in transforming the town of hay bales, gingham dresses, and "Hee-Haw" into a big-league city. Call it a finder's fee. He deserved it. He had found for Bud Adams, a man who could never win, a game he couldn't lose.

AFTERWORD:
MEANWHILE, BACK IN HOUSTON

Bud Adams has been ever tenacious in his inconsistency. In the aftermath of his Nashville deal, at various times he indicated an interest in helping Houston, where he would continue to live, get another NFL franchise. At other times, he said he would undertake nothing that involved dealing with Mayor Bob Lanier.

"I don't have any grudge against the mayor," he said in one of his conciliatory moments. "He didn't think there was any sentiment out there to help the Oilers, and he was right. He didn't think we would really leave. I was 71, and the lease had three more years to run. I believe he thought the city could put off doing anything about the Oilers until the lease ran out. But I wasn't going to wait around and fall farther behind."

On one count, he was right. "He caught me by surprise," said Lanier, "when he popped me with an ultimatum with as long to go on his lease as he had."

In Houston, football has never been city business. Roy Hofheinz, a former county judge, or chief executive officer, had built the Astrodome as a multi-purpose facility with funding from Harris County. Adams was originally a partner in that project but pulled out before construction was completed. He later feuded with Hofheinz over his rent when he did eventually move the Oilers into the Dome after a stretch in Rice Stadium. In the normal course of events, Adams would have taken his campaign for a new facility to the county.

But Adams needed Lanier, a mayor who enjoyed enormous personal popularity. A wealthy real-estate developer who was Adams's neighbor in River Oaks, he had been elected on a pledge of improving city services, and he had delivered. The crime rate had been cut significantly since he made good on a promise to put more police officers on the streets. Derelict neighborhoods were no longer ignored. A city still wobbly in the knees as a result of the oil bust of the '80s righted itself as the energy industry recovered and the local economy diversified. It regained some of its confidence under Lanier's administration.

The mayor's popularity swept the spectrum of the community, and a project on the scale Adams envisioned was nothing more than a fantasy without Lanier's backing. If anyone could marshal support for public funding of such a scheme, he could. Lanier was never entirely convinced that anyone could.

"Even putting me at my maximum skill and maximum charm, which is fairly low," Lanier said, "man, he would've been a hell of a load.

"You need the sports community, the business community, the media, and the public behind it. He had none of those. He was relying strictly on me to get things done. One reason I get things done is I don't attempt things that aren't possible."

The mayor did mount a considerable effort, however, after choking down some of the bile that rose from the idea of putting public dollars into a private sports enterprise.

"Initially, I was outraged at the arrogance of these sports-team owners," he said. "I never was then and I am not now of a frame of mind that sports facilities should be my No. 1 priority. I told Bud and the others from the outset, 'This is not a deal I'm going to head; it's not my No. 1 priority. You need a consensus, broad-based community support.' I had to work through my own anger toward the owners for trying to shift to the taxpayers the burden of their own incompetence as labor negotiators.

"These owners fashion themselves as the jungle animals of the free enterprise system. In reality, they're the pussy cats of a monopoly world, and the characteristics of a monopoly are high prices and low service. If they had to do business in the real world with their methods, they would all go broke. If they couldn't look to the taxpayers to bail 'em out, they'd run their businesses and quit doing stupid labor contracts."

Other than those trivial concerns, the mayor felt warmly toward Bud's designs. Lanier did come around, in fact, to throw his weight behind a publicly funded baseball stadium for the Astros of Drayton McLane, Jr. One of the significant differences was that the project enjoyed support in all of the sectors Lanier had outlined to Adams. Under the leadership of Ken Lay, chairman of Enron Corp., the business community pledged to raise $75 million toward funding of new facilities for all major pro sports, a sizable portion of which was designated for baseball. The project was developed on a county-wide basis rather than being left to the city, which has half the tax base of the county. No taxes that would otherwise have gone to basic services were used and the measure passed in a referendum.

"And I thought the baseball deal had a chance to give real sizzle to downtown development," said Lanier. "With baseball, you're talking about 80 dates. Football is only 10 a year, and they're on Sundays.

"I've changed my position somewhat," Lanier said. "I still think it's outrageous, but that's Congress's business. They did it that way."

Bud Adams taught Houston that it can't exist in a vacuum. When other cities are falling prostrate before owners, those that have big-league franchises must fall in line or step down to minor-league status. The ramifications of such a demotion are subject to debate, but in a city that ranks as a regional economic center, below the world-class level of New York, Chicago, and Los Angeles, the fear factor can't be denied.

And there's little time for equivocation. In Nashville, a tier or two down from Houston, the issue appeared clear-cut: The NFL was the ticket to the big time, even if, in Lanier's words, "It hasn't made Green Bay into Paris." Is it worth it to Nashville? "It's worth it," said Lanier, "if the voters vote for it."

Nashville beat out Houston on another front as well. In June 1997, the National Hockey League rejected Houston as a site for an expansion franchise and awarded one of four to the Tennessee city, which finally got a tenant for the arena it had built on spec. Hockey was to arrive in Nashville for the 1998-99 season, a year ahead of football. All of a sudden, Possum Holler was Opossum Center, a sports hotbed, complete with competition for the entertainment dollar.

Houston's bid was said to be impeccable except for one disqualifying factor. There was no firm plan in place for a new basketball/hockey arena. Rockets owner Leslie Alexander had rejected a 50-50 split of revenues generated by events such as concerts and ice shows, throwing negotiations into a stalemate. Those seeking a hockey franchise for the city vowed to pursue a failing enterprise looking for a new home, but once again the facility had been the key.

Houston split almost down the middle on baseball. The stadium measure passed with 51 percent of the vote. In the case of the Oilers, it was never nearly that close. The city wanted football; it didn't want Bud Adams. The suggestion most often heard was to keep the team and ship him to Tennessee. It sounded good until you considered the possibility of getting Nashville to go for that deal.

When Adams proposed his Bud Dome, it was presented as a football/basketball facility, viable only if the Rockets agreed to joint tenancy. Given Alexander's subsequent intransigence with regard to splitting revenues with an NHL franchise, it hardly seems startling that he declined to share a building with a football team. He did, however, at least appear to consider the proposition for a time, and perhaps Bud had his hopes up.

As Lanier recalled, "Adams just had this child-like faith I could make Alexander do whatever I wanted him to." The Rockets owner would later prove as malleable as a rabid rhinoceros, but in this case he kept his own counsel until he visited San Antonio and took in an NBA game in the Alamodome. At that point, he said what amounted to, "Not no, but hell no," to the Bud Dome.

"Right after the legislation went down," said Lanier, "Adams sent me an ultimatum. I rejected it. The Oilers had repeatedly told me their deal would not work unless the Rockets came in. Another thing was that Adams is so unpopular that it had to be a real good deal or it would go nowhere. I'd call up people in the business community to see if they wanted to help and I'd get a dial tone. Adams sent me this ultimatum and he was 2-14 that year. I said at 2-14 he might think about going back to Jeppesen Stadium (a rickety structure on the University of Houston campus the Oilers had used in their formative years in the AFL). That seemed to irritate him, but I said it in good humor.

"When I heard he was going to Nashville, I heard he was going for an open-air stadium. I said to his lawyers that if he was talking about an open-air stadium patterned after Charlotte, which cost $165 million, I thought we could do that in Houston. When I said that, he waffled for a long time. If he'd called my bluff, it would have been hard as hell to do.

"Adams sued us (to keep Houston interests from interfering in his effort to get a deal elsewhere), then he said in Nashville that Houston is just too hot. Well, there was a chart in the paper comparing Houston's weather to Miami and Nashville, and Houston wasn't any worse. The Cowboys do pretty well with their version of an open-air stadium. But Bud never would talk to us about an open-air stadium.

"I made a major effort. Maybe it wasn't along the lines they liked or maybe my personality wasn't the best, but I spent a major portion of my time on this. I went to Cleveland and Cincinnati to look at stadium plans. I went to two league meetings and told Tagliabue we'd do an open-air deal along the lines of Charlotte. Adams could have made his open-air deal in Houston. It wouldn't have been as good a deal as they made him in Nashville, but he could've had a stadium in Houston."

Adams's Bud Dome proposal called for him to put up about $65 million. "He was willing to do his share on the plan," said Lanier. "He just never had a plan that would work. The deal with the Rockets could have been struck. Open-air à la Charlotte could have been done. I never got a deal from the Oilers that was doable. If I had, I would have gone with it."

Bud got his $292 million stadium in Nashville and a guarantee of 65,000 seats sold for every home game for 10 years, along with all revenues from concessions and parking and other events held in the facility. Lanier got an education. In 1994, a 2-14 year, the Oilers made $2.8 million according to *Financial World* magazine. Lanier took that number to the NFL owners' meetings, along with the Oilers' audited financial reports to the league.

"It was the coldest audience I ever spoke to," the mayor said. "If you're standing up there telling 'em you're not going to give 'em $100 million and Nashville will . . . I didn't get a rousing ovation, I'll tell you that. But we blew 'em out of the water on Bud's contention that Houston is a bad football town. That argument died."

Not that it mattered. "These sports teams have the best PR machines in the world," Lanier said. "They really do a marvelous job of couching issues in ways favorable to themselves. The NFL PR machine undertakes to personalize the issue — between the team and the mayor. That's big-time pressure. I'm 70 years old, I've got my living made, and I'm term-limited, so there's only so much pressure they could put me under, but for others it would be tough. They lead the discussion away from the mechanics of what's happening and make it a deal of, 'If the team stays, you win.'"

If he had the process to do over, Lanier said, he would have eyes only for Bud. He spent most of his time talking to Adams's representatives. "He came into those meetings only occasionally," the mayor said, "and then he wasn't tightly informed." While word circulated on the talk shows and on the street that Adams and Lanier had become locked in a clash of egos, the mayor maintained the issue was never personal for him.

"I don't dislike him as of this moment," he said of Adams. "As a host, he's very charming. In business, he can be pretty chicken and petty, but I really think the Oilers have been better off over the years when he has been involved in running the team, and I'm probably one of a very few people who would say that."

As for the threat that the city will pay more to replace the franchise than it would have cost to keep the Oilers, Lanier wasn't convinced. "If right now we did an open-air stadium," he said in the summer of 1997, "it would probably cost a fraction of the Bud Dome. Let 'em be gone and we can do a Charlotte deal after we have baseball and basketball taken care of. Markets don't just go in the same direction, and when one has been headed in one direction for a long time, that's often an indication it's about to change.

"What has happened to make this go in a different direction is the public has got a bad taste in its mouth with the combination of Michael Irvin, Dennis Rodman, Bud Adams, and Art Modell. Right now, if neither side put up any money, [pro-stadium people] wouldn't win an election in any city. As it is, the pro-stadium side usually spends around $1.3 million to $50,000 for the opponents, and then it just barely wins. You look at the approval ratings of the owners, and there are dead people more popular than Bud."

A person's image is often enhanced when he becomes a corpse, of course, but in the matter of comparisons to Adams, that's probably overkill.

Some believe that while Adams remains the point man for the franchise, he has already signed over ownership to his two daughters — his only son took his own life years before — and that they see the team only in terms of the cash it can generate. They rarely attend games and would hardly be inconvenienced if the Oilers played in Nashville or, for that matter, in Babylon.

Whether that assessment is true or not, Bud's hand might have trembled when he signed those papers in Nashville, but emotion was not the overriding issue at the bottom line. On the other hand, for some who had given their best years to a team and a city, feelings weren't easily dismissed.

For 14-year veteran Bruce Matthews, a Pro Bowl regular despite hopping around the offensive line from guard to center to tackle and back to guard, pulling up stakes wasn't so easy. In June 1997, the Oilers conducted their last practice at their Houston facility, which once again was regarded as the worst in the NFL.

"A lot of the younger guys are excited about going to Tennessee," Matthews said, "but, to tell you the truth, I haven't felt that excitement yet. I'm a Houston Oiler, and no matter how many years I play in Tennessee, I'll always be a Houston Oiler.

"I've got a lot of fond memories of the years I've spent at this place. When some guys would sign with other teams, they'd tell me how nice their facilities were and what a dump this place is. But you know what? I've grown to kind of like this place. It may be a dump, but it's been my dump."